Day Paddling
Narragansett Bay

Day Paddling Narragansett Bay

A Complete Guide
to the Alongshore Waters
for Canoeists and
Kayakers

Eben Oldmixon

BACKCOUNTRY GUIDES
WOODSTOCK, VERMONT

Copyright © 2004 by Eben Oldmixon

First Edition

Library of Congress Cataloging-in-Publication Data has been applied for.

ISBN 0-88150-606-0

Maps by Paul Woodward, © The Countryman Press
Book design and composition by Faith Hague
Cover and interior photographs by the author
Illustrations by the author

Published by Backcountry Guides, an imprint of The Countryman Press, P.O. Box 748, Woodstock, Vermont 05091

Distributed by W. W. Norton & Company, Inc., 500 Fifth Avenue, New York, NY 10110

Printed in the United States of America

10 9 8 7 6 5 4 3 2 1

To Carmen: Thanks for saving my life.
To Rick: Thanks for the loan of your boat.
And to Kermit, Jennifer, Richard, and Clare at The Countryman Press: Thanks for your enthusiasm and for making the production of this book a joy.

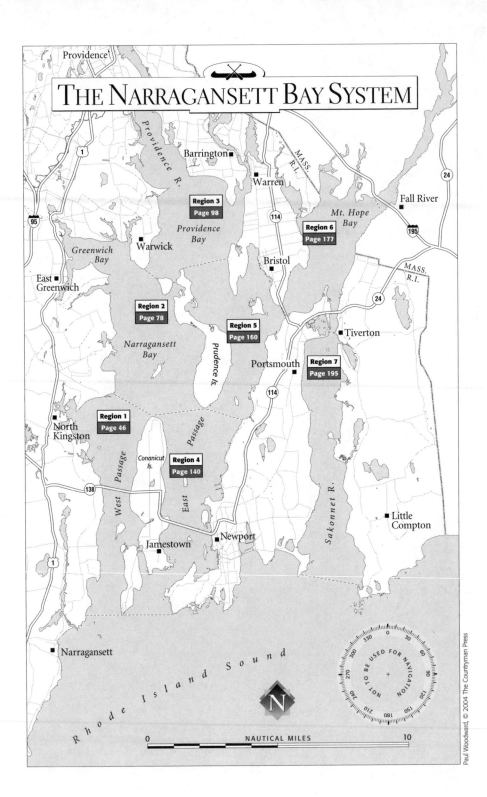

THE NARRAGANSETT BAY SYSTEM

Providence

Barrington

Warren

Providence R.

MASS. R.I.

Fall River

Region 3
Page 98

Providence Bay

Warwick

Region 6
Page 177

Mt. Hope Bay

Bristol

Greenwich Bay

East Greenwich

Region 2
Page 78

Region 5
Page 160

MASS. R.I.

Narragansett Bay

Portsmouth

Tiverton

Prudence Is.

Region 7
Page 195

North Kingston

Region 1
Page 46

Conanicut Is.

Region 4
Page 140

Sakonnet R.

Little Compton

West Passage

East Passage

Jamestown

Newport

Narragansett

Rhode Island Sound

NOT TO BE USED FOR NAVIGATION

N

0   NAUTICAL MILES   10

Paul Woodward, © 2004 The Countryman Press

Contents

PART 1

Introducing Narragansett Bay

HOPE ISLAND sits near the middle of a 3-mile-wide "inland sea" in the western portion of the Narragansett Bay system. A shellfisherman in a boat who was raking the bottom off the island's coast once remarked to me: "If you stay out here long enough, you'll see everything," and I've yet to be disappointed. The waters can be still or swift, and the waves may be 10-foot swells rolling northward from an offshore low and breaking along 100 feet of crest. Or there may be no waves at all, with the sun and clouds reflecting from a perfect, liquid mirror. The shores may be almost anything you can name, from cliff to pasture to piling. The fish you see may be smaller than a fingernail or longer than your boat is wide. The next bird overhead may be the commonest herring gull or a less usual American oystercatcher (see p. 164) or black ibis.

Narragansett Bay is far from being the largest estuary on North America's Atlantic Coast. It is scarcely half the size of Lake Champlain, which lies between New York State and Vermont with its northern tip at Canada; several Lake Champlains would fit into Chesapeake Bay, that great north-south-oriented estuary of the mid-Atlantic Coast bordered by Maryland and Virginia. Narragansett Bay, however, is more complex than Lake Champlain; that lake tapers off southward to a narrow tail of fresh water, but the mouth or, better, mouths of Narragansett Bay meet

Place-names

Let's acknowledge it. Narragansett Bay is place-name challenged.

For example, though many of us grew up convinced that Newport, Middletown, and Portsmouth are on Aquidneck Island, maps now would have us believe these towns to be on the island "Rhode Island" in the State of Rhode Island, and adding "and Providence Plantations" to the state name clarifies nothing: "What plantation"? In this book that big island is Aquidneck.

Nothing can be done, however, about the fact that Aquidneck Island has one Gould Island offshore to the west and another to its east; they could at least have been designated Small Gould and Tiny Gould or Southwest Gould and Northeast Gould, but, no, both names are the same. Conanicut and Prudence Islands both have a Potter's Cove. There are Sandy Points on Potowomut Neck in Warwick, along the east shore of the chubby southern part of Prudence Island, and along the east shore of Aquidneck Island halfway up the Sakonnet River, plus a Sand Point along the east side of Warwick Neck. We have several Long Points, too, one in Goddard State Park on Potowomut Neck, one in Wickford Harbor, and another on Prudence.

Necks and points of land around Narragansett Bay often form well-behaved combinations, as they should: If you paddle to the end of, say, Warwick Neck you arrive at Warwick Point; Poppasquash Neck, Poppasquash Point; Bristol Neck, Bristol Point; Rumstick Neck, Rumstick Point. Arnold's Neck, however, is far over to the west in Apponaug, and Arnold's Point is on the northwest coast of Aquidneck, and there must be a dozen necks without a point and points without a neck, too. Then consider Potowomut Neck: four points, Long, Sally Rock, Sandy, and Marsh, and not a Potowomut Point among them.

Compass directions may have once been dandy when it was hard to move from one island to another and each was its own little world, but you may wonder, "southwest of what?" when Southwest Points appear on both Hog Island and Conanicut. Northeast Point is on Prudence Island, Northwest Point on Patience, and North Point on Poppasquash Neck.

So, do not hesitate to ask for clarification or to use a map when seeking directions.

the North American Basin of the Atlantic Ocean. There are places on the bay where, at least in theory, you could either stand or float and shoot a bullet along a great circle course that would not cross another shoreline until it reached Australia. If the thought of "open water" ever is going to instill some respect in a kayaker, this should be a sufficient distance to do it. You may sometimes wonder how far the waves you encounter in the bay have traveled.

As an indication of its complexity, along the north-to-south axis of the bay in a distance of less than 20 nautical miles (NM), it is not uncommon on a summer day to find warm and serene coves in the north while coamers (see appendix's glossary) roar and pound into the bay's triple mouths, the West and East Passages, and the Sakonnet River.

Paddlers working their way eastward and westward across the different regions of the bay also may meet various conditions. Toward the middle of the passages through the bay, the wind tends to be stronger, the waves bigger, the current faster, and the boats or ships speedier, more massive, and more numerous. In some places in the bay, this central zone is quite narrow, as where a shipping channel well marked by buoys threads through broad shallows; in other places, it spans almost the entire width from shore to shore.

Routes described in this book have been laid out to avoid the bay's mouths and channels; instead, they go along its shores for dozens of miles of what I hope will be safe and pleasant paddling for you.

The Regions of Narragansett Bay

This book divides the Narragansett Bay system into seven regions that provide a convenient way of looking at the bay, organizing the shoreline, and planning your routes. I've drawn some boundaries between regions where risk is high, and each paddling route I describe stays within that region and does not cross into another.

These regions also convey geographical and hydrologic reality; within the Narragansett Bay system there are bodies of water with noticeably different character. Easily distinguishable are the Sakonnet River (in the past, it was known as the Sakonnet or Seaconnet Passage)

and Mount Hope Bay. The East and West Passages, too, are readily iden-
tified, at least as they pass on either side of Conanicut Island. As the East
Passage continues up between Prudence and Aquidneck Islands it retains much of its character, although it does become increasingly re-
mote from Rhode Island Sound. A good case could be made for keeping
the entire length of the passage from Castle Hill to Poppasquash Neck
together as a single region. However, the 14 NM from Castle Hill to the
north end of Bristol Harbor seemed unwieldy for trip planning and so
was divided somewhat arbitrarily at the level of the south end of Prudence Island. North of Poppasquash Neck and the north end of Prudence Island, one of Narragansett Bay's inland seas (formerly called
Providence Bay, a useful old name I use throughout this book) stretches
3 NM to the Providence River, which in turn retains characteristics of
the bay for another three NM beyond that up to Field's Point. The
Providence River south of Field's Point plus Providence Bay combine
to make another Region. Finally, another inland sea, called Narragansett Bay itself on some maps, lies west of Prudence Island, north of
Conanicut, and east and south of the mainland of Kent County (minus
its north end and including the northern tip of the Washington County
coastline). This plus the stocking cap of Greenwich Bay and its appendages together make a region.

The regions are numbered and described from south to north, then
west to east.

Region 1: Lower West Passage

Region 1 comprises the Lower West Passage from its mouth between
Boston Neck on the mainland and Beaver Neck on Conanicut Island
northward eight NM to a line between Quonset Point and Conanicut
Point. All of this stretch is relatively narrow; immediately beyond, the
distance west to east between shores from Quonset to Prudence increases to three NM. Its constrictions, the narrowest being the 0.86 NM
between South Ferry and the west side of Beaver Head, force the tidal
flow to rush through this long bottleneck at a respectable speed and to
scour the bottom to depths of consistently more than 40 feet in the
channel and locally, as off the south end of Dutch Island and near the

east ends, the highest parts of the Jamestown bridges, to more than 70 or 80 feet deep.

The wave action in the lower quarter of the West Passage, for example, up to Bonnet Shores, takes its cues from whatever is happening out on Rhode Island Sound, and on occasion that means that 8-foot-high swells roll up nearly the entire breadth of this part of the West Passage.

Farther up the passage the channel divides to pass closely around Dutch Island and then hugs the west side of Conanicut Island before petering out as it approaches the north end of the island and the unnamed inland sea.

The parts of the West Passage that are out of the path of waves from the sound and the channel's currents are within Dutch Island Harbor (once known as Fox Hill Harbour, long ago) and along the west shore north of South Ferry.

Region 2: *The Upper West Passage or Narragansett Bay*

Region 2 of the bay, which may be called Narragansett Bay or the Upper West Passage, is a large, shallow inland sea with two wide openings in the south from both the West and East Passages and just one narrow opening in the north into Providence Bay. Level with this opening, Greenwich Bay and Cove form a long stocking cap that curls west and then south. Relatively little fresh water enters the bay in Region 2, despite half a dozen streams that flow into it. The amount of new oceanic water introduced with each tidal cycle is almost nil, particularly in the upper reaches of Region 2. Although salt water sloshes back and forth in Greenwich Bay and Cove with the tides, that area is sensitive to local water quality. There's gentle paddling and lovely scenery along the mainland coast on the west side of this region. Some fine views can be seen along the west coast of Prudence Island, too, but paddling to that area involves risks and effort exceeding the skill levels that pertain to this book.

Region 3: *Providence Bay and Providence River*

Region 3 of Narragansett Bay goes from the north end of Prudence Island to Field's Point in the Providence River; it is a classic estuarine trumpet, with the Providence River as a narrow mouthpiece and the expanse from Warwick Neck to Poppasquash Neck as the opening of its flared bell. It measures 7.3 NM from Field's Point to the north end of Prudence Island and 3.0 NM from Warwick Neck to Poppasquash Neck. It is surprisingly straight, aligned along approximately 351 degrees magnetic. Unlike a smooth trumpet shape, however, Region 3 shows periodic constrictions that make it appear on the map to be a chain of lakes. The greatest expanse of open water in the Narragansett Bay system unpunctuated by any islands, even a sandbar, is the inland sea formed—reading clockwise starting from the north—by Nayatt Point, Barrington Beach, Rumstick Neck, Bristol Neck, Poppasquash Neck, the north end of Prudence Island, Warwick Neck, and, jumping across the Providence River, back to Nayatt Point. This "sea" used to be called "Providence Bay"; it is roughly circular and about 3 NM in diameter.

Next to the north in the "chain of lakes" is a nearly circular "lake" 1.7 NM in diameter, a part of the Providence River pinched between Gaspee Point and Bullock Point (0.8 NM apart) at the upstream end, and downstream between Conimicut Point on the western shore and Nayatt Point on the eastern shore (0.9 NM apart).

About 1.2 NM farther upstream, Sabin Point juts into the river from the eastern shore; Pawtuxet Neck is directly across from it but does not protrude to form a point of land, so there's not as pronounced a constriction of the river at this point as between the paired points downstream.

Finally, Field's Point, 1.25 NM farther upstream, protrudes from the west to close off half the river's width. North of Field's Point the entire width of the Providence River is given over to the Fuller Rock Reach and then the Fox Point Reach of the shipping lane into Providence Harbor.

Waves, especially those created by a south wind, come charging up into Region 3 through the 1.3-nautical mile–wide gap between Prudence Island and Poppasquash Point. Between Warwick Point and Northwest Point on Patience Island, you'll meet smaller waves, although you'll still be entertained by them. Points of land that enter these waters, such as Rocky Point, Conimicut Point, and Gaspee Point on the west shore and Nayatt, Bullock, and Sabin on the east, can provide shelter remarkably well. On a day when flags are standing out stiffly to the north and the waves south of Rocky Point are rolling over your kayak's cockpit, the water in Rocky Point's lee may be almost glassy. This circumstance, though, cuts two ways: Even on days with a breeze, there's likely to be sedate paddling to be had along some stretch of shore in this region, but conversely, wind, wave, and current can pick up dramatically as you venture out of the lee of a point.

Winds sweeping up the East Passage into Region 3 can be like a squall sweeping the length of a large lake. Watch the flags: When they begin to stand out from the poles, waves can build quickly. The tricky part about waves in this region is that they often come from more than one direction at once. This means that different waves demand different steering and balancing responses. It also means that they reach your boat at irregular intervals. Thirdly, thanks to constructive interference, some waves will be nearly twice as high as the typical wave; expect occasional 2-foot-high waves from trough to crest. Of course, thanks to destructive interference, there will be, at times, comparatively calm pools of still water amid the hurly-burly. You can then get your speed back up before the next flurry.

The shipping lane should not intrude on an alongshore trip, but the lane approaches within 400 yards of Poppasquash Neck, Gaspee Point, and Sabin Point, and less than 100 yards from the eastern shore south of Field's Point. Merchant ships are far larger than sailboats and other usual bay craft: Stay far away from them.

Region 4: Lower East Passage

Without any islands such as Conanicut, Aquidneck, or Prudence from Bristol south, the bay would be a squarish plain of water about 9 NM east to west and maybe 12 NM north to south, not the net of passages and inland seas that exist today. Triangular Aquidneck, however, rests its northern tip almost upon the eastern shore at Tiverton and sprawls farther and farther to the west across the bay as you look south. Castle

Hill in Aquidneck is a scant 3 NM from Boston Neck, yet it's 7.5 NM from the eastern border of the bay at Sakonnet Point. Not only does Aquidneck's asymmetry restrict access to the western bay, but Beaver Neck, the south end of Conanicut, occupies the middle of the 8-NM-wide gap between Castle Hill and Boston Neck.

The outline of Conanicut in the south appears to bear some relationship to the shapes of the shores to its west and east. The shore of Boston Neck runs north and south and the opposed west side of Conanicut from Beaver Head to Beaver Tail does as well, and where the southwest tip of Aquidneck slopes away to the northeast along the side of Newport Neck, the southeastern points, Beaver Tail, Lion Head, and Short, Southwest, and Bull Points, fall right in line to mirror that cross-channel cliff, and leave, out of all the breadth of water there would have been without the islands, a mere 0.5 NM between the rocks of Bull Point and the side of Newport Neck. It is much the same on the west side of Conanicut in Region 1: 1.2 NM from Boston Neck to Beaver Neck, 0.8 NM from South Ferry to Beaver Head.

Constrictions cause currents to accelerate and to scour, and they must have done so here in Region 4 in earnest, for the character of the main channel through this region is alarming. Two hundred yards off Castle Hill you'll find the greatest depth (more than 180 feet) in the entire bay and in most, if not all, of, Rhode Island Sound. Between Fort Wetherill and Castle Hill rushes the fastest tidal current in a broad channel in the bay; according to the charts it reaches 1.3 knots.

The point is that in Region 4 the channel must be entered only with great care.

Region 5: Upper East Passage

Region 5 is the portion of the Narragansett Bay system between the east side of Prudence Island and the west sides of Aquidneck Island and Bristol Neck.

Farther down the bay from Region 5, in what this book calls regions 1 and 4, the West and East Passages on either side of Conanicut are approximately comparable stretches of water, each about 1.3 NM wide on average, bottlenecked at the south, widening out in the north, each with a deep, well-defined channel that occasionally throws out a loop to encircle an island, as around Dutch Island in the West Passage and Rose Island in the East.

Above Conanicut, however, there's a big difference between Region 2 west of Prudence Island and Region 5 to the east.

All the water from the West Passage and (by a quick homemade estimate using current and depth charts) a third of the East Passage's flow passes into Region 2, where it spreads out and relaxes in Narragansett Bay, whose depth at low tide is almost uniformly 20 feet across an east-west transsect almost 3.0 NM long.

However, two-thirds of the East Passage's water in Region 4 jams into Region 5 through a bottleneck 0.9 NM wide between Prudence Island and Dyer's Island and Aquidneck, and out of that, the bulk of the water goes between Prudence and Dyer's, where it digs a nautical mile of shipping channel out to depths of more than 100 feet only 300 yards from shore. Think of this, incidentally, should you get the urge to paddle down the southeast shore of Prudence.

Of course, a bay kayaker who plans a trip to take advantage of the tides could be carried along that shore by currents on flood or ebb estimated to approach 1 knot, and locally greater speeds should be anticipated.

For this book's purposes, only the shore along Aquidneck is considered, and of that, only the part north of Dyer's Island, the channel-maker, as the remainder seems to pose risks.

The strait between Bristol Point and Bristol Ferry across the water on Aquidneck (a ferry ran where Mount Hope Bridge is now and predated 1777) peels away probably better than a third of the water coming up the East Passage and rushes it up into Mount Hope Bay. It does so at speeds that probably explain why there is more water deeper than 60 feet south of Hog Island and up into Mount Hope Bay than on the west side between Poppasquash Neck and Prudence Island.

When the tide is going out, a U-shaped current takes some of the water leaving Mount Hope Bay and wraps it around the north end of

Hog Island so that water between Hog Island and Bristol Neck actually flows north into the harbor.

On a flood tide, the pattern is reversed, as Poppasquash Neck peels a strip off the water moving up the side of Prudence and directs it into Bristol Harbor. That big triangular gape, measuring 1.85 NM across at its base between Poppasquash Point and Bristol Point and with Hog Island half-plugging the space between, cannot accommodate the flow; therefore, much of it makes a U-turn around the north end of Hog Island, leaves the harbor, joins up with the flow past Bristol Point, and goes into Mount Hope Bay. Paddlers may want to be aware of this oddity: it would be very sad to be swept out beneath the Mount Hope Bridge from beside Hog Island on an incoming tide.

Region 6: Mount Hope Bay and Adjacent Tributaries

Region 6 is Mount Hope Bay plus the unusual "salt lakes" at the mouths of the Kickamuit and Cole's Rivers; the lower Lee's and Taunton Rivers can be considered part of this region, too, but the watertrail avoids these areas.

The west shore of Mount Hope Bay has some of the last considerable lengths of Bristol Neck Bay frontage that remain only lightly built up; the east shore, by contrast, has become a mixture of industrial, commercial, and dense residential neighborhoods with little to draw alongshore paddlers. Most of the north shore is pleasant for paddling, but from Lee's River east to the Fall River shore there are hazards associated with the large electricity-generating plant and then the shipping channel. The south shore of Mount Hope Bay is short, running only between Bristol Ferry and Common Fence Point; each is next to one of Mount Hope Bay's dual passageways to Rhode Island Sound. Parts of this shore are pretty and are set aside as a nature preserve, but no formal public access points have been located along this shore, although casual access may be possible. The real drawback of the short south shore is that on both ends the waters turn into strong tidal races that test the skills and judgment of even experienced paddlers.

A paddler can spot boats and ships from a distance, but it often is harder to judge the strength of wind and waves 2 miles away when standing on a sheltered shore, and Mount Hope Bay has tricks to play in this regard. Mornings often see the the surface of this bay unruffled, I've been told, but after the sun has been up long enough to warm the land, a breeze begins to build. Land encloses Mount Hope Bay almost entirely as it has only two openings to the south—the narrow strait between Bristol Point and Aquidneck Island spanned by the Mount Hope Bridge, and the even narrower one at the top of the Sakonnet Narrows. Much of this surrounding land has been developed and paved, so the air above it heats up rapidly and tries to rise. As the air above land rises, air flows off the bay onto the land; other air must move in to take its place, but the only real entrance for cooler, relatively heavier air is beneath the Mount Hope Bridge. This replacement air comes through this bottleneck in a rush, the bay sucking it in like a large man trying to inhale through a straw. Around noon, I wasn't able to cross Church's Cove from Mount Hope Point to Bristol Point because of near-gale headwinds from underneath the bridge *(fig. 1)*.

Also, don't underestimate the power that waves entering Mount Hope Bay through that strait can deliver. It was one of those waves that flipped me upside down later in the same day that I met the headwind. (Consider that from Spar Island, a little sandbar approximately equidistant from all shores of the bay, a course of about 230 degrees magnetic will take you entirely over water to Potter's Cove on the west shore of Conanicut just north of the Pell Bridge to Newport; that gives a recip-

Fig. 1 *East side of Bristol Neck, off Mount Hope Point*

rocal course of 50 degrees magnetic, not an uncommon direction for the wind to blow, and a fetch of 12.0 NM.)

Region 7: *Sakonnet River*

Region 7 is the Sakonnet River, which used to be known as the Seaconnet Passage (Blaskowitz's map of 1777). Sometimes it is hardly regarded as a part of the Narragansett Bay system, but course it is; if Aquidneck Island were to disappear, the Sakonnet River would be the eastern part of a greatly expanded East Passage. With Aquidneck in place and with a gap between its northern tip and Tiverton, the Sakonnet River is connected to Mount Hope Bay by the Sakonnet Narrows (on the Blaskowitz map it's called the Pocasset River) and through that connection passes a significant fraction of Mount Hope Bay's tidal flow.

In shape the Sakonnet River comes the closest of any bay feature to a fjord: long, straight, narrow, and open to the ocean. The analogy could be pushed too far, as the Sakonnet River does not come flanked by mountains, although the cliffs and hills on Aquidneck and in Tiverton may seem high and grand when they block out the late-afternoon and early postdawn sun. It is closer to a "vik," or one of the long, straight inlets along the Baltic's shore (many now have disappeared because of the rising of the land as it recoils from the weight of its burden during the Ice Age) that cut (or used to cut) into the farmland and forests; the viks were populated by gifted boatbuilders and far-ranging sackers and traders and gave them the name we remember them by today: "Vikings."

From a recreational bay-kayaker's point of view, the Sakonnet is a giant wave tank, with Rhode Island Sound at the south end as wave generator and complete with a reflecting surface at the north end in the form of that curious west-to-east hook at the top of Aquidneck. The river even stays more or less a constant width from one end to the other, much as a wave tank would.

If the sound is not pulsing any waves into this wave tank, then the whole Sakonnet should be quiet (except, of course, for its swift tidal currents), and paddlers who bring the proper equipment and experience can revel in the miniature archipelago off the tip of Little

Compton at the east side of the Sakonnet's mouth, an assemblage more extensive and atmospheric than the Dumpling Rocks by Jamestown Harbor and without doubt among the most endearing little collections of sea rocks in Rhode Island. They even have ruins that from far away look like the statues on Easter Island.

More often than not, however, Rhode Island Sound jostles kayakers near the river's mouth more than these watertrails allow, and the question becomes whether mild conditions for relaxing paddling can be found anywhere in Sakonnet's wave tank when the sound is active.

Because of a combination of the river getting shallower with distance north from the sound and a series of points and headlands along each bank, northbound waves from the sound have usually expended almost all their energy by the time that they roll past Fogland Point, which lies a hair beyond the halfway mark upriver. Fortunately, this damping affects both sides of the river, the west bank north of Sandy Point and the east bank north of Fogland Point.

To cite the 2003 edition of the guide from the National Oceanic and Atmospheric Administration, United States Coast Pilot:

> *Good anchorage for vessels drawing up to 17 feet can be had*
> *in midriver just below High Hill Point in depths of 21 to 28*
> *feet. Although open to the southward, a heavy sea seldom*
> *reaches as far as this anchorage. In southeasterly gales the water*
> *is comparatively smooth inside the mouth of the river.*
> *Fishermen seeking shelter frequently anchor on the flats in the*
> *bight northward of Fogland Point in depths of 10 to 14 feet.*
> *(Vol. 2, ch. 6, p. 228)*

This assessment agrees with the opinion of local watermen that conditions often begin to get lively south of High Hill Point. Viewed from Little Compton at the mouth of the river, swells entering the river have appeared to break across the river's entire width at about the level of Church's Point, although a walk out to Church's Point revealed them to be breaking partway out from both Church's Point and Black Point across the river; the swells that made it through this narrow portion of the river were further weakened as they came into shallower water at about the level of Fogland Point and Sandy Point. At this same time, though, the water in the bight mentioned above was quite still.

Watertrails

The 12 paddling routes in this book are called "watertrails," analogous to "bike paths," where anyone who wants to can travel through interesting places in relative safety and comfort.

It was easy to lay out several of the watertrails based on my own past experience, and all I had to do was to go back and document routes and launching sites already familiar. Other parts of the bay that I knew are omitted from the book, because getting to them involved crossing open water and busy shipping channels. If you were to carry your kayak out to the island on the ferry you could undoubtedly have a safe and enjoyable trip around part of Prudence's coastline. The west side of Prudence too, while lovely, can be reached only by crossing traffic lanes, something that should be done as quickly as possible. This may be beyond what a less-than-strong paddler should be asked to do. The other watertrails were mapped out by studying the chart, then driving in and out along the shore to find all possible launching sites, then paddling through the area to find "links" connecting the launching sites, since I was trying to work toward the model of a "bike path" with launching and landing sites connected into a chain of paddling segments. Some segments may seem too short to make an interesting trip, while other segments are long enough to tax the endurance of a novice paddler, but we paddlers have little control if any over where launching sites will be made available. In places, there's a stretch of suitable coastline accessible from only one direction, there being no launching site at one of the ends; these places were made into "loops." The east side of Conanicut Island north of Potter's Cove and the east side of Warwick Neck south of Longmeadow are two examples of such loops. The links, loops, and launching sites are numbered and described from south to north. The distances given in the tables are for alongshore routes, which typically do run in a straight line.

Watertrail Lengths

Watertrail	Total Distance Described in Nautical Miles (NM)
1A	11.5
1B	3.7
2	13.3
3A	11.9
3B	10.4
4A	11.1
4B	3.6
5A	3.1
5B	9.6
6	12.3
7A	5.1
7B	8.0
Total Length	103.6

Watertrail 1A Distances (NM)

Link 1: South Ferry to Hamilton Beach	4.2
Link 2: Hamilton Beach to Wickford Town Beach	1.5
Link 3: Wickford Town Beach to Long Point	1.0
Loop 1: Long Point through Wickford Harbor and Return	4.8

Watertrail 1B Distances (NM)

Loop 1: Dutch Island Harbor	3.7

Watertrail 2 Distances (NM)

Loop 1: Spink Neck to Allen's Harbor and Return	1.0
Link 1: Spink Neck to Mount View	1.0
Link 2: Mount View to Sandy Point with Potowomut River	2.9
Link 3: Sandy Point to Goddard Park Beach	1.4
Link 4: Goddard Park Beach to Goddard Park Ramp	0.9
Link 5: Goddard Park Ramp to Apponaug Harbor	2.5
Link 6: Apponaug Harbor to Brush Neck	2.0
Loop 2: Brush Neck to Brush Neck Cove, Buttonwoods Cove and Return	1.6

Watertrail 3A Distances (NM)

Loop 1: Longmeadow to Sand Point and Return	3.5
Link 1: Longmeadow to Conimicut Point	0.8
Link 2: Conimicut Point to Passeonkquis Cove	3.9
Link 3: Passeonkquis Cove to Aspray Boathouse	0.9
Link 4: Aspray Boathouse to Stillhouse Cove	0.8

(continued)

Watertrail Lengths, *continued*

Loop 2: Stillhouse Cove to Field's Point and Return	2.0

Watertrail 3B Distances (NM)

Link 1: Bristol Town Beach to Warren Town Beach	2.2
Link 2: Warren Town Beach to Latham Park	5.5
Loop 1: Latham Park to Bullock Cove and Return	0.9
Link 3: Latham Park to Bullock Neck Beach	0.7
Link 4: Bullock Neck Beach to Sabin Point	1.1

Watertrail 4A Distances (NM)

Loop 1: Jamestown Harbor to The Dumplings and Return	1.4
Link 1: Jamestown Harbor to Potter's Cove	0.9
Loop 2: Potter's Cove to Conanicut Point and Return	8.2

Watertrail 4B Distances (NM)

Loop 1: Fort Adams through Newport Harbor and Return	3.6

Watertrail 5A Distances (NM)

Loop 1: Cory's Lane to Coggeshall's Point and Return	1.0
Link 1: Cory's Lane to Willow Lane	1.0
Loop 2: Willow Lane to Portsmouth Terminal and Return	1.1

Watertrail 5B Distances (NM)

Loop 1: Bristol Harbor North Ramp to Poppasquash Point and Return	4.7
Loop 2: Bristol Harbor North Ramp to Bristol Point and Hog Island and Return	4.9

Watertrail 6 Distances (NM)

Loop 1: Mount Hope Fishing Area to Church's Cove and Return	2.5
Link 1: Mount Hope Fishing Area to Kickamuit Narrows	0.3
Loop 2: Kickamuit Narrows to Kickamuit River and Return	2.2
Link 2: Kickamuit Narrows to Swansea Town Beach	2.5
Loop 3: Swansea Town Beach South on Cole's River and Return	2.8
Loop 4: Swansea Town Beach North on Cole's River and Return	2.0

Watertrail 7A Distances (NM)

Link 1: Sakonnet River, Sandy Point to McCorrie's Point	1.7
Link 2: McCorries's Point to Island Park Access Site #1	3.4

Watertrail 7B Distances (NM)

Link 1: Fogland Point to Sapowet Point	2.4
Link 2: Sapowet Point to Grinnell's Beach with Nannaquaket Pond	5.6

Selecting Canoes and Kayaks for the Watertrails

Here are some opinions.

Kayaks originated as seaworthy hunting boats for lone paddlers in the Arctic: agile, fast, stealthy, able to survive terrible conditions, with little more carrying capacity than was needed to bring a hunter and his prey back home. Just as remarkably, this was accomplished amid a harsh natural environment that was desperately poor in lumber, fabric, resins, glues, and tools, and rich only in rock, ice, and salt water. These ancestral craft were then and are today high-water marks of ingenuity in design and construction, satisfying all the demands of their intended functions superlatively.

Narragansett Bay presents maritime conditions resembling more closely those faced by the original kayakers than those for which, for example, the birch-bark canoe was designed. The extent to which the bay has tested the seaworthiness of open canoes (here, made from hollowed tree trunks and of sizes capable of carrying from 4 to 40 people) can be traced back more than 300 years in this account by Roger Williams:

> *It is wonderfull to see how they will venture in those Canoes, and (being oft overset as I have my selfe been with them) they will swim a mile, yea two or more safe to Land: I having been necessitated to passe waters diverse times with them, it hath pleased God to make them many times the instruments of my preservation: and when sometimes in great danger I have questioned safety, they have said to me: Feare not, if we be overset I will carry you safe to Land.* (from A Key into the Language of the Americas, *p.109)*

Hopefully canoeists will not take offense that I find kayaks to be preferable to canoes out on Narragansett Bay waters; even for alongshore paddling in the bay, the closer a recreational kayak hews to the ancestral design intents, the better a paddler is likely to fare. Today's kayak designs radically exaggerate some capability of the original at the cost of other capabilities; this is not necessarily a bad thing in itself, for doing so often produces a kayak able to negotiate situations that the original boats were not intended to be able to handle: whitewater kayaks capable of hurtling over waterfalls and spinning through rapids are one example. On the other hand, such boats have largely excluded themselves from the open and semi-open marine settings that were home to their forebears.

While conditions along the watertrails described in this book do not demand all the capabilities of a sea kayak, they emphatically require the ability to handle more than "flat water." Having to hold a course at an angle to the wind and perhaps multiple angles to two or more wave trains is a fact of life on the bay. Choose a boat that you're confident can make directed progress in 2-foot-high waves and 20-knot winds: If you spend enough time on the bay, you're likely to get the chance to test your assessment. If you're regularly paddling as a family with children, make sure the least capable boat in your group will be able to make progress in these conditions. A two-paddler kayak with a central passenger seat may be a solution to the entire-family-on-the-water problem, but flawless procedures to recover from a capsizing would be needed.

River paddlers expect to have to perform a variety of corrective strokes in succession and thus opt for boats with little tracking stiffness, while a bay canoeist or kayaker may have to make only one corrective stroke during a leg of a journey, but he or she may have to do it for 2 miles or more. If the boat is not helping by tracking well and reducing the demands on the paddler, even strong paddlers can become fatigued. Sixteen to seventeen feet should be the minimum length for a canoe or kayak on bay waters. Canoes should probably have keels; the triple keels seen on some large lake canoes are not required, but they certainly improve a canoe's tracking characteristics, sometimes to the point of making it hard to follow a winding salt creek.

Kayak designs can achieve directional stiffness by having a keel, too, but keelless designs can promote tracking stiffness by adding lateral area below the waterline at the bow (a "chin," here, as I do not know the proper word) and at the stern (a fixed skeg; see glossary). The retractable skeg (about three-quarters of its length from the bow) in the kayak used on the bay while researching this book did not much affect the kayak's tracking stiffness in calm conditions, as the "chin" and fixed skeg took care of that, along with the boat's 20-foot waterline. It turned out that the boat wanted to weathercock in a cross wind because even with a low afterdeck and high bow, the deep chin up front placed the center of lateral resistance below the waterline significantly foreward of the center of lateral resistance above the waterline. Dropping down the retractable skeg shifted the below-waterline center of resistance aft and apparently close to the above-waterline one, for the boat became neutral in an angling wind and wanted neither to weathercock nor to leecock (see glossary). If your bay kayak is not neutral by design, some mechanism for adjusting the below-waterline center of lateral resistance is nearly a necessity. Leeboards (see glossary) might prove useful to have onboard a canoe.

Having accumulated about as many miles on the bay in a kayak with a rudder as in one without, I conclude that either will work: A rudder can solve the weathercocking/leecocking (see glossary) and tracking stiffness problems as well as steer the boat, and conversely a rudderless boat can be adjusted to be neutral in the wind and also be steered well. Having fewer mechanisms on board means having less to break. Footpegs, usually present in kayaks with and without a rudder and usually adjustable or fixed, respectively, have broken off in both boats. Losing a footpeg in a rudderless boat is barely an inconvenience, but in a boat with a rudder it means that the paddler will probably have to raise the rudder out of the water and into the wind; if that additional windage in the stern makes the boat weathercock strongly or if the paddler cannot steer without the rudder, it would be quite possible to get into trouble.

Speed is another consideration for bay paddling, not in the context of racing other boats, but in relationship to the distances involved and the available time. A paddler might wish to explore Bristol Harbor (Watertrail 5B) in an afternoon and could cover 9 NM doing so; being able to make three knots would mean three hours of paddling and perhaps an hour or more for stopping to look at things. Another paddler might travel 5 NM away from a launching site and, upon turning around for home, find that the tide and a strong heading sea breeze may cut a full knot or more off his/her speed, meaning that he or she had better have at least a 3-knot cruising speed in order to have any boat speed at all on the return trip; if progress were to be slowed to 1 knot, the paddler would face a 5-hour paddle back.

In displacement craft, such as canoes, kayaks, rowboats, and shells, longer, narrower boats are faster: A shell is a rowboat optimized for

The Kayak in the Pictures

The long white kayak, the bow of which appears in several of this book's pictures, is shown in a full-length pose *(see fig. 2)*. It was designed and kitted as the "Patuxent 20" by Chesapeake Light Craft of Annapolis, Maryland, and built by the author and his friend Rick Rogers with minor tweaking of the lines at the bow and stern. It is constructed entirely out of mahogany plywood, plus white cedar sheer clamps and solid mahogany kingplanks and bow and stern fairings. It is covered with fiberglass saturated with epoxy and finished with Interlux white polyurethane enamel and Z-Spar Captain's Varnish. The boat is 20 feet 6 inches overall and 20 inches wide. It has a V-bottomed hull with a single chine, a retractable skeg, and no rudder. As with many V-bottomed kayaks, the hull is close to being unstable in roll when exactly level but quite solid when rocked to bring a bottom panel level: it has strong secondary stability. Its secondary stability is highly sensitive to the elevation of the paddler, and to get the boat stable enough for me to use routinely on the bay, I sit directly on the bottom, using a seatback but no cushion. Fortunately, that is not uncomfortable.

With the skeg down, the boat responds neutrally to wind and waves, not weathercocking (its skeg-up behavior) or leecocking. With considerable lateral area below the waterline at the very bow and stern and its formidable length, even in near-gale winds it holds a course as though on rails.

Turning the Pax 20 takes more than paddle work; you must get the hull to help you. With the chine on the outside of the turn well submerged and the inside chine raised, the boat carves respectable arcs, turning at about 15 degrees per stroke. Getting the boat to cant while keeping weight centered is done by (for a turn to port, say) bending forward and to the left, straightening your right leg, stretching your body's right side, and raising your left knee hard, as though you're trying to touch your left knee with your chin. It is a one-sided sit-up speed. "Boat-length" is shorthand for "effective waterline length," which is the distance between where your boat's hull starts to push water aside and create a bow wave to where the hull has finished letting the water close up again. If a hull is very fine at the bow, almost bladelike for a distance below the waterline, then the effective waterline will be shorter

Fig. 2 *The Patuxent 20's last landing, on the beach at Sandy Point*

motion, which, when put together with the paddling, makes the 20-foot kayak almost agile.

If you've ever been lulled by the bubble and plink that comes from the bows of canoes and kayaks when underway (to me it's an integral part of paddling), the Patuxent 20's silence may seem odd at first. It makes no bow wave, just a soundless ripple, and no wake either. Paddling hard changes nothing: The boat speeds up but remains silent. This is a sign of at least a small efficiency and may indicate larger efficiencies at work, for it seems that whatever energy can be put into pushing water backward is transformed into forward velocity of the kayak. It cruises without exertion at just under 4.0 knots, say 3.85 to 3.95, and trips of 14 NM that with another boat would have been allotted a whole day's trip are knocked off in an afternoon, with time out for rests, poking around, and picture taking. The Patuxent 20 has long legs and was essential to making the research for this book possible.

by that amount. Fineness of the bow and stern can make the effective waterline length shorter by several feet, so that a kayak with pointed bow and stern, plus fine entry and exit that measures 17 feet long overall, may have an estimated effective waterline length of 13 feet and is likely to feel this in the cruising speed.

"Speed," here, is not so much a hard upper limit on your boat's speed, some ultimate "hull speed," as a measure of how fast a particular hull will travel when driven by the amount of power that the paddler is comfortable producing, something like "the comfortable cruising speed." This does seem to be related to the theoretical hull speed (which in turn is related to the square root of the effective waterline length) in that the hull with the higher hull speed will move more quickly for a fixed submaximal paddling effort than one with a lower hull speed.

If you plan to range up and down the bay along these watertrails, you'll probably find it desirable to be able to cruise at 3.0 knots, which in turn means, as a rule of thumb, that you are able to paddle past a stationary object in 3.3 seconds in your 17-foot boat, bow to stern. (If your boat is 17 feet long, divide 9.8 knot-seconds by the bow-stern transit time to get boat speed in knots.) Sea kayak hull shapes will let you accomplish this quite readily, but so will other hulls.

Advocates of sea kayaks might recommend reading about boat design and selection in, for example, *The Complete Book of Sea Kayaking* by Derek C. Hutchinson. Nick Schade has written thoughtfully and intelligently on the subject in *The Strip-Built Sea Kayak*, too.

Paddlers who need to measure the capabilities of themselves and their boat against the demands of the bay may find it wise to start near the top of the bay and work their way downward; unsure of how I'd fare with my kayak in conditions near the mouths of the bay, I took a series of shakedown trips starting around Greenwich Bay and then successively farther south in the bay, tweaking and adjusting the kayak between trips. The problem solving was entertaining and satisfying, and the result was that the long, narrow kayak that appears designed more for straight-line speed on a calm lake and myself safely developed the qualities needed to negotiate the bay.

Rigging

One benefit of making your own kayak is that you feel no compunction about changing things around. You can experiment, for example, with various ways of arranging bungee cords on the decks or move the seatback or screw on a few loops of webbing where they seem needed. Paddlers in ready-made boats may have to use a finer touch than simply drilling a pilot hole through the deck into the sheer clamp, pushing in some thick epoxy, and then driving a stainless steel screw and washer holding a homemade loop of nylon webbing. But some modifications may be possible. (Just do not compromise your hull's flotation.)

The basic observation about gear is this:

"If it isn't tied on, it's going to be gone."

This applies to sponges, hats, lunch, fiddly but essential little clamping nuts, paddles, and all those other conveniences, including the biggest convenience of all, the boat itself.

Should you tie yourself to the boat? No, but make your boat as close to impossible to lose as you can, and that means having a perimeter line. You are half-conscious in the water; you flail one arm across the boat's foredeck near the bow; your cold fingers curl weakly and reluctantly; they slip across the slick wet surface; and then? The answer is to catch a line that is easy to hold on to and goes completely around the deck of the boat. You must be able to grip your boat firmly from any direction, anywhere your hand finds a gunwale.

Am I suggesting that you tie the paddle to yourself or to your boat, as well? No, again, but you ought to have something paddle-like that will get you, if not home, then at least to safety. Maybe you'll even be able to catch your dropped paddle. By the way, do you know whether your hollow, two-piece paddle floats after it has filled with water? Paddle leashes, which connect you to your paddle, do not seem practical to me, who finds himself holding the paddle far from the center, even at one end and the middle, for turning and bracing; anything that would restrict flexibility in use of the paddle seems more a risk than a benefit. The basic "paddle leash" is mental:

Always have a paddle in your hand(s).

All other items get tied on. A favorite green sponge sank into murky lake water. After recovering from capsizing I found my favorite hat was gone, despite its chin strap. The pump and the lunchbox on the after-deck (see glossary) got in the way of slithering onto the boat during the recovery, forcing an ugly choice between getting back into the boat or keeping the items. Now the loop of a bowline on 6 feet of line goes through the sponge; the other end of the line is tied to a webbing loop by my right hand in the cockpit. My present hat is attached to my life jacket by a short line. The lunchbox is on a line long enough to let me pull it into the cockpit. The pump is on another line long enough to let it be held even at the front of the cockpit opening while the paddler is seated. The fixed ends of all the lines are within easy reach, so that pump, lunch, sponge, and anything else responds to a come-hither pull.

A paddle float rates as an absolute necessity, and one usual place to keep it is rolled up and snapped under a bungee cord on the afterdeck. I now keep mine partially inflated and tied to a 15-foot line secured to the sheer clamp on the side of the cockpit from which I extend the paddle blade with the float while reentering. When it's strapped onto a paddle blade during a recovery, the paddle itself is effectively on a long leash attached to the boat, which seems reassuring. The long line makes certain that movements of paddler and paddle during reentry are not restricted. While I'm paddling, the float fits crosswise on the cockpit floor to support my thighs and knees, where it helps to steer the rud-derless kayak, because when one leg is straightened, the other is lifted into position beside the knee brace cushion. The paddle float also goes from being an item inspected once a season to one that is felt, looked at, and adjusted every trip, which is good for such a critical item.

Most kayaks have toggle grips attached by rope to the extreme bow and stern, but another Greenland-style feature has proven to be doubly useful: Two loose arches of thick line attached thwartwise a foot or so in from bow and stern serve not only as comfortable handholds, but provide places to hold down the far blade of the paddle, the near blade going beneath a bungee cord near the cockpit; the occupant has both hands free and the paddle is fast to the boat.

Tests of bungee cord configurations on the decks showed the simplest arrangement to be the best, the Greenland style of stringing cords straight athwart the deck at uniform intervals, three across the foredeck and four across the afterdeck.

Tired of having to work to keep my mouth above water when practicing wet recoveries in a lake, I opted for flotation over style by wearing a Type I (Offshore rated) life jacket, and the added ease in working around the boat during a recovery is a revelation: You can actually relax while having your face held out of the waves. However, make sure that the foam blocks in the front of the jacket do not hamper you from clambering onto the afterdeck.

Paddles

The paddle I use is long and broad-bladed; it pushes considerable water backwards with each stroke and feels as though it "locks" in the water. However, at some point after 12 NM into a trip, my forearm flinches anticipating the jerk to come when the next stroke locks into the water, and the idea of a softer, more gradual bite to eliminate the jerk becomes appealing. The mind begins to toy with a Greenland-design paddle with long, thick, narrow blades that might even support their own weight (that is, float) and bring on the resistance smoothly during a stroke.

Wrist problems may develop after kayaking, and one may wonder whether the injuries were caused in part by the common practice of using the paddle with blades rotated (typically 60 degrees) out of alignment, since that style requires that one hand firmly grip the paddle's shaft and that that wrist flex or extend in order to get the active blade in position for the next stroke. With aligned blades in calm to mild conditions, neither hand is required to grip the shaft tightly, as the forces involved are almost purely pushing and pulling, the former done with the outside part of the palm and the latter with the first phalanx bones of the first two fingers. It's less stressful to hold the upper arms vertical and the lower forearm level; the middle of the paddle makes a curved figure-8 just above the spray skirt. As waves become wilder, both grips tighten uniformly, but at least you do not have to flex your wrists. This style always presents the thin edge of your paddle's blades to a side wind, so there's no tendency for the force of the wind on the raised blade to tip the boat, as can happen with wind from any direction acting on a raised blade rotated less than 90 degrees. Once, paddling a broad-beamed boat heading into a Beaufort 9 gale, I was rotated during a paddle-stroke about the boat's long axis by the wind's force on the rotated, raised blade. With the blades in line, the boat was sometimes stopped dead by the wind, but it never tipped. Keeping the blades aligned also lets you know at a glance the orientation of the blade at the other end of the paddle. It requires no thought, and there are times in a narrow boat when being wrong by 10 degrees can flip you over, never mind being off by 120 degrees.

If a headwind picks up sufficient strength so that pushing the flat of the raised blade into it becomes real work, then you probably ought to think about switching to the Greenland-style storm paddle. This kind of paddle is so short that the raised blade is in front of your body. It presents no additional frontal area (or lateral area to tip you, either) and is always convenient to have along as your backup paddle. During the trips for this book, a storm paddle probably would have been in use a quarter of the time, had I had one.

When steering a long, narrow boat through waves, I frequently shift the paddle through my hands to left or right. My paddle's shaft has been decorated with two broad rings painted on with light-colored plastic enamel just outside of where I place my hands. In rough conditions these rings have been a great help in showing me where the paddle is being held with only a glimpse at its shaft in peripheral vision. During calm conditions, they tell when the drip rings on the paddle shaft are spaced symmetrically, for neatness.

Piloting and Navigation

Piloting is the practice of finding your way around on the water by referring to fixed earthly objects, literally landmarks on land or buoys and the like on the water. Navigation, if it refers to fixed objects at all, uses the "fixed stars"; everything else that it uses changes: time, velocity, azimuth, elevation, and so on. In the bay, piloting is the norm: A paddler sees the land and goes to it or around it. The watertrails involve the most primitive kind of piloting, since the paddler makes his or her way along relative to the shore. Paddlers can also strike out from shore across a bay or passage using only primitive piloting, too, by regarding the bay's bodies of water merely as large ponds and heading for some feature on the opposite shore. This casual approach to leaving the safety of an alongshore route can lead to tragedy. The bay is not a pond, and no one should count on always having the luxury of being able to see land. The question that the solo paddler or the leader of any group must have an answer to is: "What shall I do if I cannot see even the bow of my boat?" (This may seem an exaggeration on Narragansett Bay, but it is not one in Maine at least, where fog can be so thick that on familiar ground you stretch out your arm in front of you so as not to walk into a tree or the side of your own house.) I consider a heading compass mounted on the boat to be minimal equipment when paddling on the bay; that, and a chart.

The heading compass on a kayak should be mounted on the deck close enough to reach (they have a rotating bezel that you set to show your desired course) but far enough away to not require refocusing your eyes from looking at the waves. The ones stocked by kayak outfitting stores work well. There are compasses that one can remove from the boat, but I've had no experience with them; my preference is to have boat and compass inseparable.

You can clip a waterproof chart case to your boat, typically to the perimeter lines in front of the cockpit and keep a paper chart inside it, or simply snap a waterproof chart under the three bungee cords on your foredeck between you and the heading compass. One waterproof chart that has withstood several seasons of use is made by Maptech, Inc., their ChartKit Waterproof chart #18.1, which measures 14" by 60". This chart is essentially NOAA chart #13221—Narragansett Bay (with additional information from NOAA charts #13218 and #13223 and Maptech's own annotations about fishing, wrecks, and launching places) transferred to both sides of a material that can be rinsed off in the shower after a trip and hung up to dry. The NOAA charts themselves can be found at mapsellers' shops in the area. (They're not copyrighted, and copying services are willing to make same-sized black-and-white replicas on conventional paper. Many uses can be found for these copies as-is or annotated, and whole or cut into pieces, whether at home or in the boat.)

Knowing your probable cruising speed, your location on the chart, the direction toward your goal, the effect of wind on your boat, and, importantly, the cumulative effect of the currents between you and your goal, you can estimate the corrected heading which you should paddle in order to arrive at your goal, then use the heading compass to be sure you maintain that course. The steps involved in the estimation are fairly simple and can be done graphically on your chart; refer to any number of books on compass use and piloting of small boats. Such corrected courses, sometimes differing 15 degrees or more from the direct heading, can be wonderfully accurate. Doing nothing but hold a predetermined corrected heading it is entirely possible to arrive at a chosen buoy or rock more than a mile away. When a paddler can do this, he or she can begin to feel some merited confidence in being able to get home if rain and fog were to set in. A paddler can also return to a launching site that he or she can no longer distinguish in the land on the horizon, which can save much needless travel, time, and effort.

How to know your position on the chart is the remaining unsolved issue. Continually updating your position mentally with glances at your chart as you proceed along a shoreline is a good habit. Away from shore, a Global Positioning System (GPS) unit will give you a location in terms of latitude and longitude. Many units also will tell you the bearing from your boat to another location, such as a waypoint or the landing site. Finding a lat-lon coordinate location in the bay may take some preparation of your chart, however, as chart gridlines usually occur at 5-minute spacings, which (for latitude) equals 5 NM and is longer than most distances from land in the bay. Draw in and label additional lines over the water at one-minute intervals or less, using waterproof ink.

My favorite method of determining my boat's location does require visibility but with a little practice I find it fast and surprisingly accurate. It calls for a second compass called a "bearing compass," which you hold in your hand and sight over toward any feature that you can also identify on the chart: a hill, a tower, a buoy, a point of land. The bearing compass shows the direction from you to the object; you plot the reciprocal course on the chart from the object; your boat is along that line. Another sighting off to one side of the first gives an intersecting line, and your boat is near that intersection. A third sighting, and even a fourth, will close in on your location quickly. Since there's really no need to ever convert the magnetic direction from the compass back to a true direction, I prepare my bay charts with lines drawn in waterproof India ink aligned to 0 degrees magnetic and placed near where I intend to be on the bay. A transparent plastic overlay in the form of a square with lines radiating from one corner at 5-degree intervals (along one edge, 5 degrees up, 10 degrees up, 15, 20 . . . 85, along the other edge), a kind of coarse protractor, can be manipulated with one hand to establish reciprocal courses, among other functions. It can be easier to visualize the bearing lines rather than uncap and cap a pen or discover that the paper wrapped around china markers swells and falls off. Punch a hole through the overlay and tie it to a light line fastened to a bungee cord. A cautious kayaker might do the same with the waterproof chart.

Piloting around the bay like this adds an unexpected degree of pleasure to paddling. I hadn't anticipated the glee that came from centerpunching a buoy I wasn't able to see from nearly 2 miles away.

Risk

The paddling routes to be described are unabashedly "low risk"; not "no risk," but "low risk." (You can come to harm even in quiet water; paddling is an "assumed risk" activity.) However, many obvious risks around Narragansett Bay can be avoided.

Many craft, powered or under sail, can travel the bay while paying attention only to extremes of weather, other craft, and the depth of water under their keel. Paddlers, however, forgo the speed, power, and assertiveness of larger craft and in so doing gain by experiencing each nuance of the bay more closely and directly. The price they pay, however, is greater vulnerability and a corresponding need for alertness and anticipation of dangers.

A lot of the business of knowing where a risk begins involves correctly measuring current and future conditions against your abilities, and while some paddlers rightfully would not want to find themselves a mile from land in daytime, others might only start to feel concern when halfway to Block Island with high seas running and a full gale coming on. It is part of the fascination of paddlecraft, especially of kayaks, that these craft should be capable of combining both great fragility and great seaworthiness: How can something that could be snapped in two by a powered rubber boat round Cape Horn or cross the North Sea? Therefore, it is the job of the paddler to know, with some precision, the capabilities of boat and paddler together, to know what conditions pre-

Flipped (and What to Do about It)

At some point the bay flips everybody. Every paddler's responsibility is to know how to keep a capsizing from turning into an emergency. If you've never swum beside your inverted boat and tried to get underway paddling again, then experience it as soon as you can, certainly before your next trip. It must be a natural part of paddling for you and everyone in your party.

Canoeists have it easy. When they go over it's taken for granted that they'll be tossed from the boat; that the boat will fill with water but will stay afloat; and that they'll slosh out some water, clamber in, bail some, and then paddle until they're under way again.

Kayakers face more pressure, because everybody knows that somewhere there's a kayaker who, in the same situation, could roll back upright with the fluid aplomb of an otter. A nonroller has to get out of the boat that's holding him or her upside down, let water fill up a hitherto air-containing, if not-quite-dry, cockpit, and try to get onto and then into the rolling, slippery thing, manually pump water out of the cockpit, and get under way, all without tipping over a second time.

While there seems to be no getting around most of these steps, short of being able to roll upright like that otter, there's no reason to feel incompetent about all this, because this perfectly serviceable prosent a danger, to be able to see them in time, and to know how to skirt them and still take pleasure in the journey.

The boundaries of some risks are marked on the water by buoys, lights, and other aids to navigation. The boundaries of other risks do not appear explicitly on nautical charts, although charts give information that helps you understand where the boundaries are likely to be. There are charts of currents as well as depths, and it's good to study a wide variety of charts about the bay.

Risks move around, too: for example, other boats. A sailboat regatta that's out in the middle of the bay when you're near shore is scenic and presents no risk at all; the same regatta bearing down from starboard even when it is still quite a distance away can foretell a danger if it is spread out broadly and you intend to cross its path. In the case of the regatta, though, you'll have time to ponder whether you'll make it

cedure can be done competently; every kayaker, even rollers, will probably have to fall back upon the procedure eventually.

"Sea room" is your friend. When recovering from an upset, you don't want to worry about boulders in your lee while also having to complete a series of precise wriggles in order to be able to enter the cockpit, remove the float from your paddle, pump, and start making steerageway again. Recovering while surrounded by water for a healthy distance is almost always safer than trying to bring your boat to a rocky shore in the conditions that caused you to capsize in the first place: Kayaking magazines have told of tragedies that happened when kayakers, capsized by wind and waves, decided to try to swim with their boats to a rocky islet when it would have been better to keep where they could have recovered and started paddling again in safety. You can land your boat with far greater control when you're in it, compared to when you're beside it in the water, and landing on rocks is not a good idea at any time. If you're used to reentering your boat and getting back in control while away from shore, you'll be less likely to conclude mistakenly that any fixed object at all is safer than water.

Reality and What to Do about It

The hardest part about paddling safely on the bay may be coming to terms with what I call "The Bay Kayaker's Reality Check," which is:

"I'm the lowest, the slowest, the least visible, and the most fragile craft out here."

The only quality of these four criteria that a paddler can improve to any practical extent is visibility. (Audibility ought to be included in that, too; a kayaker always carries a whistle, but why not something louder, like an air horn?) Another paddler and I were once standing on the Wickford Town Beach and looking out over the cove, when I saw movement on the water halfway out to the point on the south side of the cove. It was the shape of a person in a dark kayak, with a black paddle and dark clothing, coming straight toward us. I pointed it out to my companion, who looked for a moment, and then added, "And there's another kayak beside that one." Imagine how difficult it would have been for a powerboater to see those paddlers. On the bay, the more white you display the better, especially if you're low, slow, and fragile.

across before the boats arrive—you just have to make the right decision. In the case of a point of land that extends into the bay, where powerboats at full throttle cut in close as they make for harbor, you may not have the luxury of time.

In the end, observing the bay continually with an experienced and knowledgeable eye and tracking the changing stamina and alertness of yourself and every person in your party is the best way to keep risks at a distance.

Tides, Currents, and Tide Tables

Water in the wild is a changeable element. If you climbed a hill last weekend, you could be fairly certain that, unless an earthquake or a large machine had been hard at work, it would still be there next weekend. Lakes and rivers will probably be much the same from one week to the next, as well, although over the course of months and seasons their levels may rise or fall in response to rainfall, drought, or society's demands. That tidal creek in the bay that was overflowing at two o'clock last Saturday afternoon, however, may not be overflowing next Saturday at the same time, and you might be hard-pressed to predict how long it would be before a Saturday-afternoon flood would reoccur.

A tide table will show you the times of every high and low tide during the year at the location you're interested in visiting. Annual tide tables are sold at marine supply stores and bait shops, for example. Tide tables can also be downloaded via the Internet; use the usual search engines and try "tide table Narragansett Bay" as a search phrase. May's tides at Conanicut Point in 2003, at the north end of Conanicut Island, for example, could be found at the URL http://www.mainehar bors.com/ri/maycon03.htm.

Even a brief inspection of tide tables for southern New England uncovers the fact that the time differences between tides at locations such as Narragansett Bay, Buzzards Bay, Massachusetts Bay, and the Pollock Rip Channel off the southern tip of Monomoy are large, considering how small a geographical area is involved, so be certain that the tide table you consult for your bay kayaking pertains to the interior of Narragansett Bay. Fortunately, within the East and West Passages, Providence Bay, and Mount Hope Bay the timing is uniform: There are no appreciable phase differences in the tidal levels. Tables for Quonset Point and Conanicut Point, two common reference points, are equivalent, as they're within sight of each other, but Newport Harbor, too, should show (nearly) the same timing.

A paddler may be even more interested in tidal currents than in details of the absolute water level, for those can significantly assist or resist his or her progress around the bay. The standard references are the annual *Tidal Current Tables: Atlantic Coast of North America* (International Marine/McGraw-Hill) and the longer-term *The New Tides & Tidal Currents of Narragansett Bay* (Rhode Island Sea Grant/Ocean Engineering). The former, annually published reference provides the times of "slack current" (the absence of current, which happens at both high and low tides) and times, speeds, and directions (that is, whether ebbing or flooding) at Quonset Point. The maximum current speed at

Quonset Point might seem uninteresting, but the way that it clearly fluctuates along with the phases of the moon, which are also shown, drives home the point that trip planners can benefit from looking at more than just the weather. Just what the tidal currents will be up to at any particular time and place in the bay is the subject of the latter reference, which contains a series of maps of the bay related to the time of high water at Newport; for example, there will be a map labeled "Tidal Currents in knots nine hours after high water at Newport, RI." Each such map shows hundreds of closely spaced arrows throughout the bay; each arrow points along the direction of the local tidal current and is labeled with the current's speed in knots. These maps provide an effective means of developing a sense of the bay as a variegated but unified system. Paddlers who would like the currents to help them along rather than carry them backward should find it useful to refer to these maps to see when and where to find a helpful current and, if none is to be had, where currents at least are not at their strongest. Usually, in a band about 10-boat-lengths wide along the shore, tidal currents are weak, although there are exceptions, so the alongshore watertrails in this book dodge most of their influence. Still, picking up a free mile or two over the course of a day trip makes a paddler at least feel clever.

Tidal current maps can also catch the interest of anyone interested in the health of Narragansett Bay. So much of the bay's well-being depends upon the responses to the question: How long will it be until this bit of waste water or runoff reaches the ocean, where it presumably can be considered Somebody Else's Problem? If you add up the current velocities over half a tidal cycle, you can estimate that new oceanic water does not reach far up into the bay with each tide: A packet of water starting at Bonnet Point at low tide, it seems, would not clear the north end of Conanicut before returning south along the West Passage, for instance. The general input of fresh water from the rivers and streams feeding into the bay superimposes an overall north-to-south motion upon this tidal sloshing, and it is this factor that strongly controls the "flushing time," or "residence time," of the bay. Consult "On the Residence Time of Water in Narragansett Bay" by

M.E.Q. Pilson of the University of Rhode Island Graduate School of Oceanography, published in the journal *Estuaries*, vol. 8, pp. 2–4, in 1985. In this article, Dr. Pilson concludes that the average flushing time in the bay system is 26 days, with a range from 10 to 40 days, shorter in wet weather, longer during drought. Whatever we pour into the bay, then, will wash back and forth with the tides for nearly a month before being released into Rhode Island Sound. How should these facts influence what we do?

Bay Temperature

Temperature strongly affects paddlers, too. It's extraordinary that Narragansett Bay and Rhode Island Sound should abut the part of the world's oceans with, to my knowledge, the very widest swing in sea-surface temperature during a year, as the Gulf Stream warms us in summer and backs away to allow polar water to cool us in winter. The high temperature occurs in August/September, the low in February/March; thus, water temperatures in May are likely to be as low as those in December. And since paddlers dress for water temperature, and not air temperature, December through May is definitely full wet- or dry-suit time.

Shallow bodies of water change their temperature with the seasons more than do deep bodies, and landmasses have a greater seasonal temperature differential than do bodies of water. So, a shallow body of water cut up by landmasses and having a long coastline, such as Narragansett Bay, must have a particularly wide swing in temperature from summer to winter and back. Would this foster more or less biological diversity?

Wildlife and Natural History

The descriptions of the watertrails will reveal that I go kayaking as much to see what nature might show me as for any other reason. Watching birds while paddling the bay gives me much pleasure. I recommend you bring a waterproof pair of binoculars along. Try a magnification around 9X: You'll be trading off the need to make out plumages of water birds at a distance against the fact that keeping an object in your binoculars' field of view from a rocking kayak becomes more difficult as magnification increases.

These field guides to birds are all excellent:

Roger Tory Peterson, *A Field Guide to the Birds* (Boston: Houghton Mifflin Company, fourth edition or later)
National Geographic Society, *Field Guide to the Birds of North America* (Washington, DC: National Geographic Society, second edition or later)
David Allen Sibley, *National Audubon Society: The Sibley Guide to Birds* (New York: Alfred A. Knopf, first edition or later).

Invertebrates (worms, clams, snails, and jellyfish) are prominent citizens of the bay, and one guide to them is:

Kenneth L. Gosner, *A Field Guide to the Atlantic Seashore from the Bay of Fundy to Cape Hatteras* (Boston: Houghton Mifflin Company,1982). Peterson Field Guide Series. This book has a short section on seaweeds, too, that's adequate for the bay.

Information about some of the alongshore grasses is harder to find, oddly enough, without resorting to pulling out the "big guns," such as Henry A. Gleason's *The New Britton and Brown Illustrated Flora of the Northeastern United States and Adjacent Canada* (New York: The New York Botanical Garden, 1952). A fine general guide to local flowering plants that you may see on beaches or in salt marshes, however, is *Newcomb's Wildflower Guide* by Lawrence Newcomb, illustrated by Gordon Morrison (Boston: Little, Brown and Company, 1977).

What I know out about the bay's geology is spotty and superficial compared to what is known to geologists. But even that little is fascinating, and anyone who follows these watertrails and also ventures into some parts of the bay's shoreline where these watertrails do not go will find the most unusual beaches and outcrops.

The Pell Library on the Bay Campus of the University of Rhode Island at South Ferry in Narragansett houses an abundance of information about the bay and its workings for the curious.

A source of information about many aspects of the natural history of the bay is the Audubon Society of Rhode Island's Coastal Education Center in Bristol; currently, its telephone number is (401) 245-7500.

The Rhode Island Canoe and Kayak Association (RICKA) has a website at http://www.ricka.org, and from there you can find information on basic safety and on advanced topics, as well as how and where to accompany groups of club members on trips on Narragansett Bay, and elsewhere in southern New England, for paddlers of all skill levels. Membership is reasonable and highly recommended, as there's a printed newsletter, plus trip notifications via e-mail.

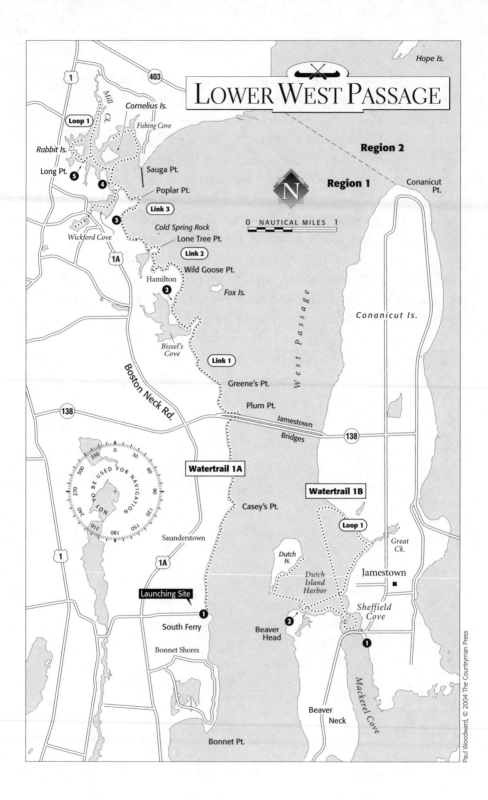

PART II

The Watertrails

Watertrail 1A:
South Ferry to Wickford

WICKFORD HARBOR, at the northern end of this watertrail, is dense with kayaks in summer, but not many paddlers try out the alongshore waters to the south that front some of the most attractive and typical, in the best sense of that word, unspoiled countryside left in the West Bay. In part, it is a matter of distance, but not being familiar with the available local launching sites may play a role as well: Starting from within Wickford Harbor, as is commonly done, puts a paddler 2 NM farther away from, for example, the scenic south side of Rome's Point than if you launched from the less well-known beach at Hamilton. If these additional 2 miles were used to lengthen a trip beyond Rome's Point, then you could visit Greene's Point, then Plum Point, the Jamestown bridges, and even Casey's Point, almost as far south as Saunderstown.

South Ferry, at the southern end of this watertrail, is a favorite launching spot for groups of experienced kayakers who may cross the

West Passage to Dutch Island, travel south along the side of Beaver Neck to Beaver Tail, cross to the west shore, and return by way of Bonnet Point. This kind of route, however, can be demanding and always depends on the waves in Rhode Island Sound. This watertrail stands as a suggestion to try an easier and more consistent, yet still scenic, route by going north along the shore from South Ferry to Wickford.

As there are no public access points between South Ferry and Hamilton Beach, the first link in Watertrail 1A covers 4 NM, even without side trips. This is not an unreasonable distance for a relaxing paddle, but some logistics are acquired to avoid doubling the distance to 8 NM by having to return to the starting point for the car. The route is attractive and interesting, though, and even without logistical support you might consider making two round trips of 4 NM, starting from each end in turn.

Watertrail 1A, Launching Site 1: South Ferry Beach

South Ferry has a deserved reputation as being on potentially demanding water, but kayakers looking for a relaxing paddle can paddle north along the western shore from there, following Watertrail 1A.

The stone jetties at the north end of the beach are remains of the ferry facilities from the days when first sailing vessels and then steamboats connected Narragansett and Saunderstown on this west shore with the west side of Conanicut Island and the east side of Conanicut with Newport. The book titled *The Jamestown Ferryboats: 1873–1969* (Wilfred E. Warren, 1976), says that ferry service between Jamestown and South Kingstown was authorized in 1873 and again in 1888, but there's no mention of when the service finally lapsed. What is clear is that on this shore Saunderstown to the north became the principal terminus. Warren says that throughout the years, the landing in South Kingstown had been known as Smith's Landing, Cottrell's Landing, Narragansett Ferry, South Landing, Landing at Boston Neck, and so forth.

From South Ferry you're able to look across the West Passage to

Dutch Island with its south end marked by a blocky white tower; the entrance to Dutch Island Harbor is south of the tower and Conanicut Island lies beyond. The U.S. Army maintained Fort Greble on Dutch Island at one time; the Narragansett Transportation Company operated a ferry called *West Side*, which supplied the fort with water. Another called the *J. A. Saunders* made the run with passengers; both vessels operated out of the Saunderstown ferry terminus. The towers of the Pell Bridge to Newport can be seen above the trees to the right of the Dutch Island tower. During summer and fall, campers and trailers crowd along the top of Fox Hill on Beaver Head in Jamestown's Fort Getty Park.

South Ferry Beach: Driving

The South Ferry launching area is at the eastern end of South Ferry Road, on the north side of the pier for the research vessel *Endeavor* operated by the University of Rhode Island's Graduate School of Oceanography at (look for signs) the University of Rhode Island's Bay Campus. South Ferry Road intersects RI 1A (locally posted as Boston Neck Road) at a four-way crossing with a traffic signal. The roadway continues on the west side of RI 1A as Bridgetown Road, which intersects US 1 at its other end, with the roadway continuing westward there as RI 138 (also posted as Mooresfield Road).

South Ferry Road reaches the shore of the bay by descending to the water at the northern edge of a band of gently sloping land between rocky cliffs to the north and south that drop straight down to the water; ready access to the bayshore, after all, must have been an important reason that a ferry service had its terminus here.

To find the South Ferry beach, get onto RI 1A somewhere between Wickford and Narragansett, go north or south as appropriate, and look for the well-marked intersection with Bridgetown Road (heading west, away from the water) and South Ferry Road (heading east to the launching site).

When coming along South Ferry Road, slow down once you reach South Ferry Church at the top of the hill. The side of the hill toward the bay becomes increasingly steep, the sightlines are limited, and the

Fig. 3 *South Ferry (from north); URI Graduate School of Oceanography's research vessel* Endeavor

pedestrian, bicycle, and motor-vehicle traffic along and across the road is plentiful and unpredictable.

The main launching area *(fig. 3)* is a beach with about 150 feet of shoreline; it is about 30 feet to the high-tide line from the front of the parking lot at the end of the road. There's another, smaller beach to the left sheltered between two breakwaters; this can also be used. The parking lot holds only about a dozen cars, and there's an emergency ve-hicle access onto the beach, which must be kept clear. Sailboats and powerboats are moved on and off through here, and it serves the needs of tow-and-rescue vehicles. Try not to block it just to launch your kayak when there's a parking space available. If there are no free spaces, you can park your vehicle in the access to off-load a kayak and then move to the first parking lot up the hill and to the left (made available through the generosity of the URI GSO).

South Ferry Beach: Launching

The view from South Ferry is wonderfully scenic and unusual even for the bay; the water is clean, the waves have an edge of ocean wildness, and the opposite shore (if you include the south end of Dutch Island), is only 0.7 NM away.

As South Ferry lies close to the mouth of the West Passage, much of the water that enters and leaves the bay with the tides flows through this narrow channel, and as the shores on both sides are rocky and dif-ficult to erode and widen, the bottom has been scoured down to a depth of more than 40 feet for most of its width.

The tidal currents at South Ferry are swift by bay standards, reaching 1.2–1.4 knots according to the chart, but some days you could swear that it moves at about 3 knots right off the end of the URI pier. Remember that tidal currents are at their least, zero actually, when the tide is fully high or low. It is fastest halfway between, that is, at maximum flood and ebb, which is midway between high and low tides (about 3 hours and 12 minutes from each).

A stretch of cliff begins south of South Ferry at Bonnet Shores and rises up to the heights of Bonnet Point. Bonnet Shores Beach is attached to the west side of Bonnet Point and faces south; where the shoreline resumes its southward run, the cliffs reappear. Across the West Passage from these cliffs lies Beaver Tail, and at this point you should consider yourself to be at the mouth of the bay and approaching Rhode Island Sound. If you know how to control your boat in coastal waters, there are beautiful sights to be seen. But this area is not where relaxing kayak trips, such as this book will describe, can be reliably found. South of the slope at South Ferry and east of Bonnet Point, ocean swells usually roll in off the sound and bounce off the cliffs in ways that should remind you that the topography of the shore can affect kayakers. Even if you wish merely to head south from the South Ferry beach to explore the slight cove immediately south of the pier, you must be cognizant of the tides, for as you round the end of the URI pier, you may encounter tidal currents capable of wresting control of a boat from a less strong paddler.

To paddle eastward from South Ferry means to head out from shore toward Dutch Island and Conanicut Island. Immediately offshore you'll encounter the channel of the West Passage with all its boat traffic, tidal currents, and, at this position in the bay, remnants of oceanic swells and exposure to wind-generated waves.

Watertrail 1A, Link 1: South Ferry to Hamilton Beach

In mid-September on a flooding tide, the clear water off South Ferry Beach is likely to be alive with at least one large school of 3-inch-long

Fig. 4 *Looking north from South Ferry along the west shore of the West Passage toward the Jamestown bridges*

juvenile herring. These will probably be harried by skipjack, which are young bluefish. The carpet of minnows sweeping beneath your boat will appear—depending on strength and angle of the light—dark and sleek, translucent like frosted glass, or bright as mirror-polished silver. An abundance of young fish is always a sign of a healthy bay.

The waters along the shore to the north of South Ferry, mile after mile, are usually moderate and inviting, and the views are superb *(fig. 4)*.

Paddle left northward along the shore from South Ferry Beach as far as you like: Casey Point is 1.3 NM to the north, the side-by-side, old-and-new Jamestown bridges to Conanicut Island are 2.4 NM away, Hamilton Beach is 4.1 NM away, and the Wickford Town Beach is 5.6 NM away. There are small beaches where you can pull boats ashore for lunch and a rest between South Ferry and the bridges and more between the bridges and Wickford. If the sound of traffic doesn't bother you, use small, clean beaches immediately south and north of the bridges themselves.

The moored sailboats among which you may pass as you paddle north from the beach are smaller and not so grand as the yachts in larger harbors in the bay, but they show a more homespun variety in design, rigging, painting, and naming. Observe them closely before heading through them; they're often all aligned, steady, and predictable, but at other times, especially in a brisk wind, they can twist uneasily and swing in all directions from their moorings. You may decide to go inshore of the boats when this occurs. It happens when wind and tidal current are moving in opposite directions: a north wind on a flood tide, a south wind on an ebb tide. When the force of the water against the boats' hulls on average nearly balances the wind's considerable force on their freeboard, cabins, masts, and standing rigging, then each boat responds to the varying resultant force upon it, swerving and pirouetting about its mooring like a colt tethered to a stake. A kayak cannot enforce a right-of-way in the best of situations and certainly not among a crowd of hulls moving mindlessly and restlessly about. Here's an example of the rule that on the bay "safe" is not a guarantee but a result that is helped along by looking carefully around and understanding what you see.

Again in mid-September, a vee of more than 50 cormorants (double-crested, perhaps) was flying south over the landward end of the bridge, possibly beginning their migration. Three stragglers flapped hard in order to catch up and "slot" themselves into the vee. The forward two tried to insert themselves into the longer, western arm of the vee, up near the front, but could not break into the line, so these two churned along behind the leading birds. The trailing straggler slipped upward to center on the right-hand outer wing of the very last bird and seemed almost to click into its proper place. This bird's wing beats slowed to synchronize with those of the others in line, making use of a vortex each bird created that benefited the one behind.

When you pass the wooded sections of the shore, watch for belted kingfishers; two russet bands across the breast denote the female, one band for the male, and both the color of a blue jay above, except with a bigger head and bill, wings farther back and shorter, and that memorable churring rattle of a call. If plentiful schools of minnows indicate a healthy bay, then the kingfisher's presence shows a peaceful, healthy shore along these waters.

On some days you may also see antique airplanes overhead that are flying in and out of Quonset. One well-known World War II trainer, North American's AT-6 or SNJ, appears frequently and is well represented by beautifully maintained specimens. You may ride in them for a fee, aerobatics extra.

As you paddle this route, try to keep within a corridor between 5 and 8 boat lengths from shore. This distance should keep your craft out of the zone of breaking waves and give you enough sea room to

Fig. 5 *Rocks between Casey's Point and the Jamestown bridges; looking south, back along Watertrail 1A*

maneuver around the various rocks and points of land *(fig. 5)*, yet keep you in whatever wind and wave shadow the shore can provide. Much of the time, heading north will put the wind at your back and pack a knot or two onto your speed. It would seem that waves should roll up principally from the south, but through some twisted physics the dominant trains of waves may come at you from the east, out of the direction of the passage's channel by the other end of the bridges. In any event, paddlers ought to be willing to regularly encounter waves more than a foot high except on the calmest of days. If you're paddling 100 feet or so from shore, even if the water should get the better of you and your craft temporarily, solid land is nearby—although all the general considerations of recovering in the vicinity of shore still apply.

You'll approach and round a nose of land, Casey Point, as you paddle north. This is another of the bay's "hollow" points, with a tidal salt pond inside a barrier beach. These places are invaluable refuges and feeding grounds for the bay's shorebirds. Gulls and wading birds are almost always at the sandbar across the pond's mouth or are farther in. A rule-of-thumb for gauging your behavior in a natural setting such as this is: "Do not cause an animal to alter its behavior." If you would like a closer look at the wildlife, you might consider taking along a pair of waterproof binoculars so that you can observe the birds feeding and resting without disturbing them.

Part of the explanation for why this stretch of water is more or less exempt from the swells and currents of the channel is that the channel bends northeast toward Conanicut north of Dutch Island, and at the western side of the West Passage, where Watertrail 1A lies, the bottom shoals upwards until at the bridges the water out to halfway from the mainland to Conanicut is still only about 15 feet deep at mean low tide; three-quarters of the way across, however, beneath the bridges' main spans, it goes down to almost 90 feet. That's quite a drop-off!

Going under the bridges should be no more of an obstacle to paddlers than the other parts of Watertrail 1A *(fig. 6)*. The areas between

Fig. 6 *Looking south along the West Passage from the south side of the west end of the Jamestown bridges*

the bridge supports are wide, although not wide enough to turn your boat around, and there almost always will be a current, though usually weak. By far, the bulk of the water moving along the West Passage has chosen to flow under the other end of the bridge and is not interested in being where you are. All paddlers have to do is choose a gap between the pier groups and confidently drive straight through right down the middle *(fig. 7)*.

On reaching the north side of the bridges, paddlers will find the

Fig. 7 *The Jamestown bridges' west ends from the north side*

change in wind and wave almost miraculous. The south wind has lifted over the bridges and will not find the bay's surface again for a quarter mile, often, and something, be it the bridges themselves, their being located at Plum Point north of which the West Passage begins to widen out into a bell mouth to the north, or the shelter provided by Plum Point, filters out awkward and demanding waves and leaves the water's surface almost serene. It is a time and place inviting relaxation and drifting parallel to shore while looking through the low ceiling of the shallow glass-clear saltwater aquarium that supports your boat.

From the north side of the bridges to Hamilton is 1.6 NM, if one cuts straight across to the beach from Rome's Point. Greene's Point, the north side of this first cove beyond the bridges, signals the beginning

Fig. 8 *View north from the cove between Greene's and Rome's Points; Fox Island in the skyline beyond Rome's Point*

of a rare and beautiful 1.5 NM long stretch of shoreline which has not yet fallen to waterfront development and extends out to the end of Rome's Point, the next prominent headland to the north, wraps around Rome's Point, jumps the entrance to Bissel Cove, and ends at the next launching site, Hamilton Beach *(fig. 8)*.

Roughly halfway around the shoreline between Greene's Point and Rome's Point *(fig. 9)* and perhaps 100 feet from shore there's a boulder

Fig. 9 *Rome's Point from the north; Jamestown bridges in the background*

which looks like the barnacled back of a surfacing gray whale; it can give a paddler quite a start as it slides by the chine, missing the paint by the grace of a providential wave.

If you are fortunate enough to be near Bissel Cove above midtide, a visit is possible; closer to low tide, almost any craft will ground outside of a narrow unmarked groove that could only be called a channel by gulls and ducks. Bissel Cove shelters at times scores of wading birds and shorebirds; entire pages out of bird guides line up nearly shoulder to shoulder along the sandy spit around which the outlet creek bends. Following the paddler's principle of least disruption and rather than scratching your boat's bottom (or, worse yet, your feet) in the shells of deceased oysters gaping up in the muck of the cove, consider landing at Hamilton Beach and taking a look into Bissel Cove from land. Paddlers attempting to enter or leave Bissel Cove at any but slack water should be prepared to have to get out of their craft and walk against the current that tears around the curving entranceway and should wear shoes to protect against cuts from shells.

Fig. 10 Hamilton Beach, sheltered between two rock breakwaters; Fox Island offshore; beyond is Prudence Island

Watertrail 1A, Launching Site 2: Hamilton Beach

The beach at Hamilton is a little treasure. Scenic and clean, it is the closest public access point to the undeveloped shoreline north of the Jamestown bridges, between Greene's and Rome's Points *(fig. 10)*.

Hamilton Beach: Driving

Drive along the stretch of Boston Neck Road (RI 1A) that connects Wickford and the approaches to the Jamestown bridges. Come south 1.2 miles from Wickford or north 1.8 miles from the approaches to the T-intersection with Waldron Road, which runs east to the water. This intersection is about 0.1 miles north of the little bridge over the Annaquatucket River, which has broadened out to a long pond decorated with white waterlilies and arrowleaf on the west side of Boston Neck Road.

Go east on Waldron Avenue, cross a small bridge over a feeder creek to Bissel Cove, which will be coming into view on your right, and bear right at the next fork in the road, onto Worsley Street; drive to the end. Several cars are usually in the parking lot between the end of Worsley and the water, but typically three to five spaces are available.

Hamilton Beach: Launching

The beach at Hamilton offers access to some of the most unspoiled paddling in the West Bay, the shoreline to the south as far as Greene's Point. If this shore could be preserved for posterity and if paddlers were permitted access to the bay somewhere between Greene's Point and South Ferry 2.6 NM away, life would be a little closer to perfect. The West Bay would be significantly friendlier to paddlers.

From Hamilton a paddler can of course continue north, but standing on the shore looking east he or she also sees Fox Island and over to the right, Bissel Cove, both features unusual enough to attract the curious. Pros and cons of paddling into Bissel Cove have been mentioned; with a personal disinclination to disturb already stressed wildlife, my verdict would be against splashing around in the cove. This is being written late in 20-plus trips along the bay's shoreline, after what amounts to a moderately systematic survey of bay shoreline, and Bissel Cove, previously just another local feature, takes on some importance as a surviving instance of a kind of sanctuary and feeding ground never numerous but now reduced to outright rarity: the shallow, unpolluted, well-oxygenated, large salt pond.

A paddler looking at Fox Island from Hamilton Beach might consider whether or not to take a closer look. Imagine that the waves are small near shore, and that the wind is light and from the south; the question is whether 0.5 NM offshore, where the far side of Fox Island lies, conditions will be the same. The 3-fathom line wraps around Fox Island, for the shoal south of Quonset Point extends this far south, although here it is drawing in toward the shore, while the mainland begins to swing east to narrow the gap between it and Conanicut. Up on this shoal the tidal current lacks the zip it has out in the channel, so from Hamilton to Wild Goose Point almost all the way to Fox Island the tidal current's top speed will be 0.2 knot and the usual speed but half of that. Close to the island, though, the flow divides, speeds up, and scoops out the bottom to nearer four fathoms in places, so a paddler should prepare for marginally stronger currents around midtide nearer the island. Psychologically and realistically, too, the east side of Fox Island can bring a feeling of suddenly increased exposure: long views up, across, and down the bay appear, the depth does increase almost at once, the south wind is stronger out beyond the shoulder of the mainland, and waves intensify in the deeper water out of the wave shadow of the island itself. Powerboats often cut off part of the angle between Wickford and the Jamestown bridges by aiming inshore of Fox Island, so paddlers must objectively assess how visible they are to fast-moving boats that may be letting down their guard after leaving busy Wickford or may be distracted by preparations for entering the harbor.

Watertrail lA, Link 2:
Hamilton Beach to Wickford Town Beach

Paddling north along the shore from Hamilton Beach, past Wild Goose Point, then to Lone Tree Point, and in to Wickford Town Beach can be done either with or without excursions in along the shores of each cove between the points, according to your whim. Dozens of boulders lurk close to shore, particularly around the points, angular enough to gnaw into a kayak's waterline. Along the bayside face of Wild Goose Point look for one of the largest boulders standing free along the shore in the

Fig. 11 *Looking south from the northeast corner of Wild Goose Point, with its landmark boulder; in the distance is Rome's Point*

upper bay, the size of one of those small overnight cottages from before the era of motels and shaped like one, complete with peaked roof *(see fig. 11)*. The shoreline formed by closely spaced points and coves weaves out and in like an amusement ride, worth doing for its own sake; paddlers intent on reaching their destination who cut across directly from one point to the next have to resign themselves to missing more than half the fun of this route.

Watertrail 1A, Launching Site 3: Wickford Town Beach

Kayakers flock to Wickford Town Beach *(fig. 12)* with good reason; the local waters are generally friendly to paddlers and interesting to explore, and there's no shortage of parking. It can be the starting point for enjoyable excursions, particularly along the 1.5 NM of shoreline between here and Hamilton.

Fig. 12 *Wickford Town Beach (left half of the photo)*

Wickford Town Beach: Driving

The beach is to the left as you enter from RI 1A, Boston Neck Road. Drive to the side road's end at a barrier, then turn left and make an S-curve into the parking area. There's a sloped walkway to the beach on the right, but in season, with all the toddlers about, it is probably better to lower your boat down the short drop to the beach farther to the left.

Wickford Town Beach: Launching

There are no special considerations of current or depth in the embayment.

The best tactic seems to be to launch in line with the property fence in the middle of the beach (northern boundary of town's section) and slowly ease out along the shore to the north.

Out of season, kayaks come and go at will along the Town Beach, but during swimming season paddlers must take special care not to mix with swimmers; the bow of even a plastic boat is harder than a child's head. Swimmers venture even to the middle of the cove, so it might be a good idea to leave this cove to the swimmers altogether, except for putting in and taking out.

Watertrail 1A, Link 3: Wickford Town Beach to Wickford Harbor (Main Street, Long Point)

Paddle north along the beach until clear of the swimming area and then continue over to Poplar Point, marked by a lighthouse and distinguished by several attractive and architecturally inventive houses along the shore. Swing wide at the point to stay clear of any rocks and breaking waves. The safest way to get through the gap in the seawall into the harbor is to curve around the near end of the seawall, leaving a margin of about 1 boat length, a maneuver which requires a controlled turn in the immediate proximity of angular boulders unsuitable for any attempts at landing and significant wave action; be sure that every member of your party is capable of this turn.

Pull up in the water in a position closer to the seawall than to the rockpile on the bay side of the southern jaw of the harbor entrance; powerboats commonly turn right leaving the harbor to pass between the seawall and the "rockpile." Move forward enough to be able to monitor boat traffic approaching the opening from both inside and outside the harbor. When there's a lull in the traffic, make your move *(fig. 13)*.

Paddling through the opening into Wickford Harbor is one of the riskier and more demanding needle-eyes in the area that a kayaker can choose to thread. Do not assume that this is a place to be negotiated casually just because there are a lot of kayaks in the vicinity.

Fig. 13 *Traffic passing through the Wickford seawall's gap*

Once inside, if you plan to cross to the north side of the channel, perhaps to go to Fishing Cove, go in parallel to the channel until well past the 5 MPH LIMIT marker buoy, then cut straight across the traffic way. Darting across the harbor opening when close to the seawall and perhaps hidden from some boat's view is not a good practice.

To reach any of the launching/landing sites that terminate Watertrail 1A, move closer to the southern shore inside the seawall and continue eastward (about 105 degrees magnetic) to the point where one spur of the channel splits off to go south across your path into the busiest part of Wickford Harbor. Using due care, go straight across the traffic lanes to a small mooring ground bordered by a long wharf on the south and a beach ahead to the west: The south end of the beach, close to the wharf, is Launching Site 4, at the end of Main Street. Branches of the channel are north and east of this sheltered water.

To reach the other launching sites, paddle out the north side of the mooring ground and continue along a row of floating docks, then past some buildings; you'll be going north-northwest. Between two of the buildings, Pleasant Street comes north from Main Street to end at the water in a ramp open to the public but not described here.

Farther along to the west is one of the most popular launching sites for paddlecraft and small powerboats in the harbor—the public ramp in Wilson Park at the end of Intrepid Drive on Long Point. Either continue paddling alongside the channel moving from one point of land to the next until you arrive at one with a paved ramp coming down, or look for the pair of buoys that straddles the channel—"green can 9" and "red nun 10"—cross the channel from one to the other, and go farther into the harbor along the north side of the channel; the ramp will be clearly visible at the end of a headland ahead and a little to the left.

There's a floating platform to the right of the ramp as you face it from the water. The usual place to put in and take out kayaks and canoes is at the left edge of the ramp, where there's some sandy footing between the ramp and some rocks.

Watertrail 1A, Launching Site 4: Main Street Beach

The little beach accessible from the end of Main Street in Wickford introduces a kayaker directly into the middle of the harbor, but from within a buffer zone protected from boat traffic *(fig. 14)*.

Fig. 14 *Kayaker with a small sit-on-top kayak, starting out from Wickford's Main Street Beach*

Main Street Beach: Driving

Approaching Wickford from the north along US 1, turn left after the police station on the left and at traffic light onto RI 1A toward the heart of Wickford. This part of RI 1A is also Main Street. When Main Street reaches the business district of small shops, RI 1A turns right, while Main Street continues ahead past mixed historic residential and small-business frontages. Follow Main Street; it ends at a parking lot ahead and to the right and a small unpaved roadway to a seafood concern ahead and slightly left. The lane to the beach begins a few feet along this second entranceway, on the far side of a hedge.

Entrance to the beach is a short two-wheeltrack lane past a hedge and before low wild roses that border the business's parking lot on the left arm of the "Y." Park in lot on right arm of "Y."

From the south, come through Wickford on RI 1A running south to north. At the north end of this segment, RI 1A makes a T-intersection with Main Street. Turn right onto Main Street and follow directions above.

Main Street Beach: Launching

This beach faces a small mooring area that is in the angle between two arms of the harbor channel. As you go straight out from the beach, the trafficway into the central part of Wickford Harbor crosses your bows and extends south, to starboard. The harbor may readily be entered from here by keeping to the side of the trafficway and optionally ducking through the line of yachts lined up bow to stern along the right side of the channel farther along to avoid the harbor traffic.

To visit quiet parts of the harbor, like Fishing Cove and Mill Creek, go north parallel to the shore from the beach until you encounter the channel and the pair of buoys "green can 9" and "red nun 10." Cross quickly and explore the other side at leisure.

Watertrail 1A, Launching Site 5: Long Point (Wilson Park, Intrepid Drive) Ramp

The Long Point Ramp in Wilson Park off Intrepid Drive in Wickford is the launching site situated closest to the calmest waters in Wickford Harbor.

Long Point (Wilson Park, Intrepid Drive) Ramp: Driving

Coming south along US 1 (Post Road), watch for Intrepid Drive on the left, a small street through wooded frontage; a police station is just beyond on the left and beyond that a traffic light where RI 1A (Main

Street) goes left into Wickford proper. Follow Intrepid Drive, but slowly: bicycle paths cross at several places. When encountering forks in the unpaved section of the road, bear right. The unpaved road arrives at the rear of a parking area; drive around counterclockwise to the front left corner, where the ramp goes down to the water on the right.

It is normal for there to be nearly continual activity launching and recovering powerboats and using trailers on the ramp, so to launch or recover a kayak one most conveniently parks on the right-hand verge at the top of the ramp. There's a suggestion of a beach between the ramp and the rocks to the right (looking down the ramp) that makes a good staging area for loading and unloading the boat, too.

Parking for vehicles without trailers is on the far side of the parking area, alongside where you drove in.

Long Point (Wilson Park, Intrepid Drive) Ramp: Launching

There are no special considerations in the immediate area, other than to avoid powerboats coming to and going from the ramp and floating platform; people often fish from the point to the left, too, so you may have to synchronize your paddling with their casting.

Watertrail 1A, Loop 1: Long Point to Mill Creek, Fishing Cove, Wickford Harbor, and Return

The water is extremely tame near Long Point. Currents and waves are rarely factors.

Moving to the left from the ramp along the side of Long Point, the paddler enters an angle between the point and the west side of the harbor, which extends north about 0.2 NM and becomes an increasingly narrow salt creek. Up in here there's a small islet on which junipers and other trees have arranged themselves with the near-perfection of a monastery garden. The creek eventually becomes too small to navigate, so depending on how far you have ventured upstream and the size of your boat, you may find yourself backing out around curving muddy banks, but that is just good fun.

Standing again at the Long Point Ramp, but this time looking to your left, you'll see the entrance into an arm of the harbor called Mill Creek *(fig. 15)*. This more resembles a tapering, short river; a paddler can go about 1.1 NM from the ramp to the place where the creek starts as a rill trickling down a rocky streambed.

As you enter Mill Creek, you'll find yourself between an island on the left, Rabbit Island, and a neck of land, Calf Neck, on the right. Paddling around the back of Rabbit Island will bring you to the small salt creek just described.

Emerging from Mill Creek and keeping close to Calf Neck will bring a paddler around into a shallow passage between Calf Neck and an island to its southeast, Cornelius Island. If instead of paddling into this gap you continue across its opening and along the southwest face of Cornelius Island, you'll draw closer to the channel and boat traffic. The south tip of Cornelius Island is sandy and steep; the current can be brisk along here and keeps the channel well dredged and clean along this shore.

Going either through the gap between Calf Neck and Cornelius Island or around Cornelius Island to the south and up its eastern side brings you into the shallow expanse of Fishing Cove.

Fig. 15 *View from the vicinity of the Long Point Ramp toward one of the mooring grounds*

Around low tide even a canoe can go aground in Fishing Cove. The north half of the seawall across the harbor's mouth extends southward from the end of Sauga Point, Poplar Point's opposite number. Also extending from the tip of Sauga Point, just before the base of the seawall, a sandbar reaches almost to Cornelius Island, and it is on this that kayaks often come to a stop; back off and try again, this time closer to the island.

To continue this tour of the harbor, find a pair of buoys toward the Fishing Cove side of Cornelius Island, "red nun 10" and across the channel "green can 9"; they're close to the south end of Cornelius Island, but a little way toward the harbor entrance. Cross the channel here and bear to port, moving alongside the channel as it heads south and then branches off more to the southwest into the main harbor. This channel branch passes between wharves on each side. After the wharf on your starboard ends, a line of yachts moored bow to stern will start; on the other side of this line of boats is space that you can have nearly to yourself and not have to share with larger craft. Slip between the lined-up boats and make your way farther into the harbor *(fig. 16)*.

This protected area that you are in curves to the right and later ends before becoming a stream that flows out of a tidal pond on the other side of RI 1A through downtown Wickford. Before this, however, the boat channel turns left and parallels RI 1A, which itself turns left at the other end of town and crosses the water on a pale green steel arched bridge, a local landmark, as Boston Neck Road.

Fig. 16 *Looking north-northeast along the channel inside Wickford Harbor*

Watch for boats maneuvering in this tight area; paddle to the bridge and underneath to find either a quiet pool or an aquatic classroom filled with kayaking instructors and students.

If the tide is high, then you can paddle through the gap in the stone wall on the other side of the pool into Wickford Cove; the shallow salt pond is beyond. At low tide it's the feeding hour for herons and egrets, and they should be left to wait for incautious fish in peace. It probably will have been 10 hours since their last good meal, and even a great blue heron, a master at conserving energy whether flying or standing still, must become irritable at having to wait for the tide to fall; that may explain why one quite peevishly snapped up a large blue dragonfly that perched on a leaf too close by.

On your way back, if you are returning to the Long Point Ramp, again cross the channel at "green can 9" and "red nun 10" so as not to get squeezed between channel and docks.

Watertrail 1B: Dutch Island Harbor Circumnavigation

*P*ADDLERS, do yourselves a favor: Go enjoy Dutch Island Harbor. The water is clean and green. The harbor is usually not busy with boat traffic, compared to Jamestown (Watertrail 4A, Loop 1) and especially Newport (Watertrail 4B, Loop 1) Harbors. Waves here have been almost nonexistent even when the West Passage was seeing swells from distant hurricanes. The wildlife is a revelation and delight, especially what seems to be the resident loon which while not tame is inquisitive and free of fear if a paddler sits quite still *(fig. 17)*.

Fig. 17 *A loon that kept the paddler company between Great Creek and the West Passage shore*

Watertrail 1B, Launching Site 1: Sheffield Cove

This is a convenient entry point to Dutch Island Harbor and in particular to what amounts to a very shallow, thoroughly sheltered salt pond, Sheffield Cove, where beginning kayakers could play without encountering anything more than mud and shells.

The main issue here is whether or not the tide is in. Even at low tide, you can walk out far enough to find enough water to float a loaded boat, but once you are underway, you may have to curve around to the right to avoid a sticky mud bar straight out from shore.

Sheffield Cove: Driving

Drive south on Conanicut, following signs to Beavertail State Park and Fort Getty. If you have come over the new Jamestown Bridge, take the Helm Street exit at the end of the bridge, then follow its weavings until you have a chance to turn right (south) onto North Road, which comes from under an overpass to your left. Follow this to Mackerel Cove, a long narrow inlet with a town beach to the left; Sheffield Cove will be on your right. The town of Jamestown charges $10 for nonresidents to park in the beach parking lot; do not park on the roadside. Launch not from the beach but across the road into Sheffield Cove, which connects to the harbor. There's a path between the rose bushes and a ramp of sorts.

Sheffield Cove: Launching

This inlet is sheltered and mild under almost any conceivable condition. The only consistent problem facing a paddler is running aground before reaching the mouth of the inlet, which conveniently opens onto the inner side of Dutch Island Harbor.

Watertrail 1B, Launching Site 2: Fort Getty (or Beaver Head or Fox Hill)

This is an excellent entry point directly into a protected harbor with many natural attractions.

Fort Getty (Beaver Head) Ramp: Driving

Continue south beyond the Mackerel Cove Parking Lot and take the next right turn, marked by a sign to Fort Getty Park, which is a community-run park, not a state park, and collects a fee for entering or for launching a boat: $10 to launch a boat without a boat trailer, $14 to launch with. Pay attendant at gatehouse. Drive straight along the main road of the park, which bends right, then passes trailer campsites on Fox Hill to the left. Just beyond is the landing ramp to the right, a beach suitable for launching to the left, and a fishing pier at the end of the narrow lane straight ahead. Some parking spaces along the beach are designated as being only for vehicles with trailers; cars carrying kayaks or canoes on top can find space nearby on the left or right that doesn't block the lane.

Fort Getty (Beaver Head) Ramp: Launching

A small beach to the left of the ramp, when standing at the top of the ramp and looking down, may provide the most convenient launching and landing from this location *(fig. 18)*. The ramp itself is often occupied. The beach on the left (west) side of the lane to the pier also serves

Fig. 18 *View over well-sheltered, small beach beside Fort Getty boat ramp*

well but may be taking waves from the West Passage. Beaver Head, north of Fox Hill and west of the launching site, presents a rock cliff to the water of the West Passage, and the tidal currents along its outer edge match in speed those in the West Passage's main channel at this level. Trips south of Beaver Head are led several times a season by experienced kayakers, so it is possible to explore the side of Beaver Neck in the company of strong paddlers with practice in judging conditions and also in assistance and rescue. Some of these trips go to Beaver Tail at the mouth of the West Passage and beyond, where the not-quite-oceanic conditions in Rhode Island Sound prevail.

Watertrail 1B, Loop 1: Dutch Island Harbor

As launching conditions at Fort Getty vary less with the tide than at Sheffield Cove, the following description of Dutch Island Harbor starts from there and moves counterclockwise around its edges, first, and then back to Fort Getty through the mooring area. We call this place "Dutch Island Harbor" because "Dutch Island" is what shows up on the transoms of local boats, but on an old map the harbor was called "Fox Hill Harbour," after the hill on Beaver Head. That makes a kind of sense, but leaves the question of why "Beaver Head Harbor" never caught on, or why the name "West Ferry" never started.

Driving into Fort Getty Park beyond the gatehouse, on the right there's a brief view of a salt marsh and creek posted as a wildlife refuge. From the launching ramp this marsh and inlet stretch away to the right, but although it looks and is interesting, paddlers who respect the rights of certain places and their plants and creatures to be left alone will restrain themselves from entering there.

Paddle instead across the narrow arm of the harbor where you are, or go more to the left to zigzag among the anchored boats. You are making your way circuitously or more or less directly toward Sheffield Cove, which at one place backs up to the end of Mackerel Cove and where you'll find the alternate launching site. Count on seeing shells, egrets, and homey scenes of houses nestled into the woods beside the marsh grass.

After poking around in Sheffield Cove, move out along its northern side.

As you begin to head north along Conanicut again, take notice of the buildings and wharves. These are due west of the center of the Jamestown Harbor waterfront on the east side of the island. There's a promontory that sticks out to the west, and this used to be the terminus on the west side of Conanicut Island, still called West Ferry, and it was linked to East Ferry on the Jamestown Harbor side by Narragansett Avenue, a straight road which still exists, although the ferries have not run for almost forty years.

Farther up the shore the traces of the island's settled past are fewer, but the water near the shore is clean and rich: Here's where the minnow schools began in earnest and one late summer afternoon they were so continuously dense that to a person looking through the surface there appeared to be a single river of fish. If all of the minnows had been brought straight up to the surface, they surely would have made a carpet of fish, perhaps with some jiggling and wriggling into position. Since the harbor is about a mile by half a mile (whether nautical or land mile makes little difference for this suspect calculation), it covers about half a square mile. There being 640 acres in a square mile, there may have been about 300 acres of tightly packed minnows in the harbor that afternoon.

Fig. 19 *Entrance to Great Creek, the salt creek leading to Round Swamp*

Continue along the lovely shore to Great Creek, the salt creek that reaches in to North Road *(fig. 19)*. It is long and scenic but narrow and can have a swift tidal current. Paddlers who decide to venture all the way up it to where it goes beneath North Road, Conanicut's central north-south road, should bear in mind that the roadway has, not a bridge, but a sluiceway of sorts, quite capable on a flood tide of suctioning in a small boat's hull from several yards away. A loon floated by the entrance to this creek and barely had to move to feed; it dipped its head and neck into the water, flipped a minnow into the air, caught it, and swallowed, repeatedly, without pause and must have dispatched 20 minnows while I watched. North of the creek and farther along the shore, other loons were using the more conventional means of getting their food by diving.

Continue to explore northward up the shore, where it is still undeveloped and intriguing. Beaches here would make a good place to lunch and rest. At one place, though, the shoreline bends and there you are: alongside the West Passage channel and looking straight up the bay at the deep end of the Jamestown bridges. For this watertrail it is suggested that the paddler turn here. Immediately beyond one meets the full power of the West Passage confined for whatever reasons to flow principally along this shore.

Having turned and started south, the choice of course arises. Due south magnetic (180 degrees magnetic) cannot be faulted, as it should be both safe and scenic, taking one through Dutch Island Harbor's mooring grounds inside of the 3-fathom line. Extended to the south side of the harbor, this course brings one into the mouth of Sheffield Cove .

To head directly to Fox Hill *(fig. 20)* is to skirt the side of Dutch Island and to twice cross the loop of the West Passage channel which is slung around the east side of Dutch Island with the current, waves, and boat traffic that implies. Moreover, a paddler would be cutting the channel obliquely and exposing him- or herself to the traffic for almost the entire 1 NM distance, which not only would be unsafe for the paddler but would be an imposition upon powerboat operators, who would have to watch for the narrowest profile of your slow, low craft.

If you decide to visit Dutch Island, consider doing it by starting

Fig. 20 *View on peninsula's west side, opposite from ramp, looking past Beaver Head*

from buoy "red nun 2" which is north of Beaver Head; it is 0.25 NM from the buoy across the side-channel to Dutch Island on a course of 320 degrees magnetic. Reverse the course to 140 degrees magnetic to come back, starting from the small cove above the island's southern tip.

Watertrail 2: Spink Neck to Brush Point

WATERTRAIL 2 begins on the north side of Quonset Point around Allen's Harbor and Spink Neck. Paddling is easy from Spink Point on the north side of Quonset Point all the way north to Sandy Point at the south side of the opening into Greenwich Bay, then west around the point to Greenwich Cove, north to Apponaug Cove, and then along the north border of Greenwich Bay as far as Brush Neck Cove beside Oakland Beach.

The possessive is being dropped from "Allen's Harbor" on signs and maps, but since Martha will probably retain possession of her Vineyard for some time to come, Mr. and Mrs. Allen, whoever they may have been, should be allowed to keep their harbor. The "spink" in "Spink Neck" may refer to an old name for a wildflower, *Cardamine praetensis*, a member of the mustard family; it's also called "bitter cress" and grows in temperate latitudes throughout the Northern Hemisphere. Perhaps local residents gathered greens on Spink Neck while their cattle grazed on Calf Pasture Point.

The watertrail follows the coast north to Mount View, a launching site, then continues to Pojac Point where it turns west up the Potowomut River, called the Hunt River farther upstream. After leaving the Potowomut, the trail turns north to Sandy Point, a launching site, bends west to follow the southern shoreline of Greenwich Bay to Sally Rock Point, turns south along the shoreline of Goddard Park to the park's beach (a launching site) and optionally to another launching site at the boat ramp farther into Greenwich Cove. The route then runs north along the western shore of first Greenwich Cove and then Green-

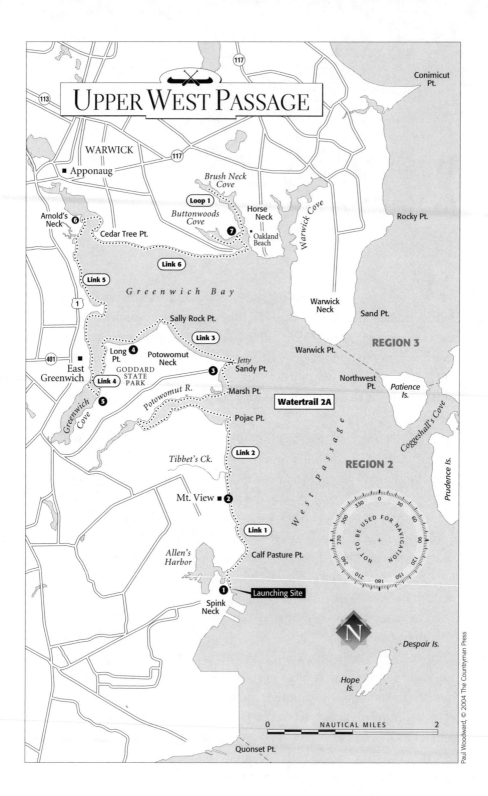

UPPER WEST PASSAGE

113

117

117

WARWICK

■ Apponaug

Brush Neck Cove

Loop 1

Buttonwoods Cove

Horse Neck

7

Oakland Beach

Warwick Cove

Rocky Pt.

Conimicut Pt.

Arnold's Neck 6

Cedar Tree Pt.

Link 6

Link 5

1

Greenwich Bay

Warwick Neck

Sand Pt.

Sally Rock Pt.

Link 3

Long Pt. 4

Potowomut Neck

401

East Greenwich

GODDARD STATE PARK

Link 4

5

Greenwich Cove

3 *Jetty* Sandy Pt.

Marsh Pt.

Potowomut R.

Pojac Pt.

Warwick Pt.

REGION 3

Northwest Pt.

Patience Is.

Coggeshall's Cove

Prudence Is.

Watertrail 2A

Tibbet's Ck.

Link 2

Mt. View ■ 2

Link 1

Allen's Harbor

Calf Pasture Pt.

W e s t   P a s s a g e

REGION 2

NOT TO BE USED FOR NAVIGATION
0 30 60 90 120 150 180 210 240 270 300 330

1

Launching Site

Spink Neck

N

Despair Is.

Hope Is.

0   NAUTICAL MILES   2

Quonset Pt.

Paul Woodward, © 2004 The Countryman Press

wich Bay to reach into Apponaug Cove (also a launching site). Leaving Apponaug Cove it turns east to follow the northern shore of Greenwich Bay to the opening just before Oakland Beach that leads to Buttonwoods Cove, Brush Neck, and Brush Neck Cove, which it explores, ending at the beach in the Warwick City Park at the end of Brush Neck. This trail, from Spink Neck to Brush Neck, can be from 9.9 NM to 19.6 NM long, depending on the extent to which one ventures into the various coves and the Potowomut River. Even Greenwich Cove can be skipped in paddling from Sandy Point to Apponaug Cove, cutting about 1.2 NM off the trail's length. This route crosses no main boating or shipping channels, although it does encounter several marinas in Greenwich Cove and outside of Apponaug Cove.

With seven launching sites and a total of about 110 parking spaces along its length on a typical day, this trail offers superb opportunities for groups of paddlers along much of its length.

In addition to the launching sites and the sheltered waters of the coves and Potowomut River, there are pleasant places to pull ashore along the trail; five come to mind, but as always paddlers should observe the guideline "Make no bother, and leave no trace."

Watertrail 2, Launching Site 1: Spink Neck

The ability to launch from Spink Neck has been a great asset to shellfishermen over the years and although I have never met another paddler heading out from there, it has been a choice entry point for kayaking the waters west of Prudence Island. It is, for example, just the place to start and end a game of "Island Tag" in which the solo kayaker keeps himself amused by trying to pilot with compasses and chart the shortest round trip which will allow him to physically pat Conanicut, Prudence, Despair, and Hope Islands. (Aim for less than 9 NM.)

Construction in the Economic Development Area, it appears, may cut Spink Neck off from the public, which would be a pity. This must be a fluid situation, and interested paddlers should hope that this fine, and rare, access point is preserved.

Spink Neck: Driving

Enter the "economic development" area of Quonset Point and follow the straight access road to its end at a gateway into an automobile off-loading and storage yard. You will have passed signs mentioning Allen's Harbor on the left shortly before this. Turn left before the gatehouse, and follow the road along the holding lot's fence and then past a few marine businesses until you see a gravel drive. Turn right and enter the parking lot by going to the end of this drive and turning left. There are several places to park that will not interfere with the area's activities.

On the north side of the end of Spink Neck is a sloping beach with a parking lot above it and a beach and rock jetty to the east. In past years this parking lot and launching ramp have been used by shellfishermen and other harvesters of the bay, and the beach and jetty have been favorite spots for sunbathing, swimming, and fishing, but the Rhode Island Economic Development Commission has erected an unwelcoming sign; despite the sign, the area is still lightly but steadily used

Fig. 21 *Launch area at Spink Neck, facing the channel into Allen's Harbor*

by members of the public as it long has been. It's up to you whether you wish to use Spink Neck *(fig. 21)*.

Elsewhere in Allen's Harbor there may be public parking and water access; their existence is indicated on at least one map.

Spink Neck: Launching

Kayakers will find Spink Neck an excellent starting point for visits to Conanicut, Prudence, Hope, and minuscule Despair Island, which all lie within reach and can all be visited in one looping trip. That journey involves crossing some of the bay's wide main channels and dealing on occasion with wind-generated waves and attenuated oceanic swells and determined tidal currents, for instance at the south end of Hope Island on a flooding tide.

Heading south along the shoreline takes the paddler around Quonset Point to Wickford, but the trip is almost 3.8 NM long (Quonset is big!) and tedious. It offers no attractions to look at and can subject the paddler to strong uneven wave action where swells that have traveled directly up the lower West Passage (Region 1) steepen as they pass across the shallows in front of Wickford and encounter the high, flat seawall on the south face of Quonset Point, away from which they reflect and rebound southward as far as the Jamestown bridges. For a small boat the area is a laboratory that teaches constructive and destructive interference of waves and delivers the lesson: Do not pass closely in front of the seawalls of Quonset Point. This obstacle of Quonset Point is enough to discourage a paddler seeking a smooth ride from extending Watertrail 1A (from South Ferry to Wickford) any farther north; in this book paddling between Wickford and Allen's Harbor or Spink Neck will not be recommended.

Watertrail 2, Link 1: Spink Neck to Mount View

Just north of Quonset Point with its airfield, docks, acres of new cars, and present extensive construction is a narrow, twisty channel between Spink Neck on the south and Calf Pasture Point on the north which opens out into Allen's Harbor, a sheltered salt pond about 0.5 NM long north to south although only a third as wide east to west.

Launching to the north from Spink Neck is technically easy, as the ramp area is well sheltered from the bay by an outstretched arm of rocks. However, remember that you must immediately cross a boat channel in continual use.

Optionally, explore Allen's Harbor, but be alert and exercise caution. It is best to hug the Calf Pasture Point shore when entering and leaving and to be prepared to encounter yachts maneuvering to stay in the channel.

Proceed north along the shore of Calf Pasture Point. At low tide, there will almost certainly be someone wading in the water off the Point collecting shellfish. You may hear warblers singing in the trees onshore: yellowthroats, yellow warblers, and more at times keep up a constant chorus among the red cedars spaced comfortably through the grass and thickets. American and snowy egrets are common in the area, of course, along with green and great blue herons, and every so often something more unusual will appear: a glossy ibis or a little blue heron. Birds regard Calf Pasture Point as a sanctuary, thanks to its seclusion.

As you move north and begin to leave Calf Pasture Point behind, you encounter an assortment of boulders connected to the shore by a stony tongue which is uncovered at low tide, when you'll have to swing wide around the end of the rocks; at high tide you may be able to pick your way through between the boulders and shore. Whatever the tide, the heights of these rocks seem random, so there's always at least one rock closer to the surface than the bottom of your boat: Be sure to find it with your eyes and not your hull.

The launching and landing beach at Mount View is north of the tongue of rocks and immediately south of a row of houses close to the shore.

Watertrail 2, Launching Site 2: Mount View Beach

Although there's never room for more than two vehicles here, and often only one, this is a perfectly located starting point for an exploration of the Upper West Passage from Quonset Point up to Warwick and over to Prudence Island.

Mount View Beach: Driving

Somewhat south of where Frenchtown Road meets Post Road (RI 1A) and the Amtrak railroad tracks pass beneath it, at about 6200 Post Road, Essex Street goes east; follow it to a "Y," take the left arm of the "Y," which is North Quidnesset Road, and go to the end.

There's parking for no more than two cars, and only on the left side beyond the end of the pavement.

Mount View Beach: Launching

Paddling close to shore north or south from Mount View is delightful. Heading out across the West Passage to Prudence Island is also one of the great pleasures of the Upper West Passage, but the previously stated cautions still apply, because conditions can switch from intense heat and glassy water to a wave-ripping squall in less time than it takes to get to shore. Think, if you're heading out from the safety of shore, what you would do if fog, rain, or darkness erased the shoreline from view. Consider the benefits of having a heading compass installed on your boat.

Watertrail 2, Link 2: Mount View to Sandy Point

Between Mount View and the mouth of the Potowomut River are no particular rocks, currents, or obstacles *(fig. 22)*. You pass in front of the Potowomut Country Club and its beach, which is a favorite hangout for representatives of whichever species of gull happen to be in the area. Schools of minnows and young herring meander along in these shallow waters and attract gulls and terns from above and bluefish from below. If you can drift into the middle of such a school of fish, listen to them patter like raindrops on water.

The land on the southern side of the mouth of the Potowomut is Pojac Point. A sandbar extends northeast from the point, and at low tide even a kayak may have to enter the river near the middle of its mouth so as not to go aground.

The Potowomut River *(fig. 23)* is one of the prettiest locations in the bay and can be reminiscent of English countryside. It is also a valu-

Fig. 22 *Shore between Mount View and the Potowomut River seen at low tide*

Fig. 23 *The serene, secluded Potowomut River*

able haven for wildlife. If we are hungry, we can go to the cupboard, but if a kingfisher, say, is hungry she must hunt for food right then and there, and her food is skittish and flees from our paddles and boats long before we arrive; kingfishers fly away from us not just because they fear us but more because we have spoiled their fishing by our presence. Having even a few boats along the river probably means the kingfishers and their families all go hungry. Two egrets, one American, one snowy, protested my approach by leaving. Three cormorants departed, too, but for inconveniencing those I felt, whether I should have or not, no remorse. A belted kingfisher passed behind my head and gave its rattle of alarm and complaint. It's difficult to step so softly that nothing moves, but it is a worthwhile goal, especially in a de facto wildlife preserve such as this. A yellow warbler continued singing off to my left; he did not object to my visit. Upriver, belted kingfishers shuttle among their favorite

Fig. 24 *Sandy Point from the south, from outside the mouth of the Potowomut River*

fishing perches on trunks and limbs that overhang the water: I prefer to leave them in peace.

Return to the Potowomut River's mouth *(fig. 24)*. The northern side of the river's mouth is Marsh Point, where there are remnants of old walls and inshore from them a small tidal pond with copious but shy shorebird life. Egrets and least terns feed from the tidal pond. (Least terns are the ones that appear to have wings too small to lift their body; they flap industriously to fly. However, this does not stop them from dueling with each other like miniature "Top Guns.") Look in from the open water if you can (high tide is best) but leave the birds in peace and do not try to paddle in.

Proceed north to Sandy Point. Approach the beach at a right angle to the shore, not alongshore, as there's a small rock breakwater at the south end of the beach; swing a good 20 yards wide of the exposed end of the breakwater so as to miss the submerged boulders there.

Watertrail 2, Launching Site 3: Sandy Point, Warwick

Sandy Point in Warwick is "Old Reliable," because no matter what the weather, there's always some excursion one can take. Good weather invites trips out to Prudence or down to Calf Pasture Point. This spot, along with the beach in Goddard Park, are the starting places nearest to the south side of Greenwich Bay.

Sandy Point: Driving

Follow signs from Post Road to Goddard Park by driving along Ives Road, but proceed beyond the park's entrances to the road's end, where there's a parking lot for 10 cars. This place is popular for fishing (off the breakwater at the Point's tip), picnics, playing in the sand, and soaking up the sun.

Sandy Point: Launching

Launch and land at Sandy Point near but not quite at the south end of the beach, which is in front of the parking lot; the very south end of the beach is steeper, has more shells, and is guarded by a small rock breakwater, and 30 yards or so from it conditions are milder and usually kinder to your boat.

A sign at the parking lot warns of strong currents and undertow, but paddlers will find these waters unexceptional and mild. Fishermen anchor small powerboats in these shallows to try for skipjack, flounder, and scup.

The waters southeast of the beach at Sandy Point are shallow (3 feet at low tide) and clean with an even, sandy bottom, so this could be just the place for a group of kayakers to go to tip over their boats and try to get back in, being careful to stay in water shallow enough to let them walk the boats back to shore if all else fails.

If your paddling experience has been on gentle rivers, calm ponds and lakes, and sheltered harbors, in other words "flat water," these are excellent training waters for bay paddling, more so east and south of the beach than to the northeast and beyond, especially progressively farther from Sandy Point, for there a paddler enters the stretch between Sandy Point and Warwick Neck, which has fast boat traffic, diverging channels, and usually a nasty chop. However, from the beach to the mouth of the Potowomut and up to a quarter mile from shore the waves behave themselves but bring enough variety to prompt you to develop the knack of having one eye always on the water one to several paddle lengths away. Farther away and that wave probably is not about to affect your boat. Closer than a paddle length, and you are in the realm of instant coping and reaction; the wave has slipped inside your envelope of anticipation and is part of your present, not your future: you have no choice except to deal with it.

Watertrail 2, Link 3:
Sandy Point to Goddard Park Beach

Launch a safe distance from the rocky breakwaters at either end of the beach, and move offshore to gain maneuvering room. Head north toward the tip of the point, but swing wide of the visible rocks, as there will be submerged rocks for another 10 or 20 yards farther out.

Turn left when past Sandy Point and paddle westward along the south shore of Greenwich Bay. The water is less than 2 fathoms deep, and the bottom is sandy, clean, and even, but there are several submerged rocks scattered through this area *(fig. 25)*.

About halfway to the next point of land there's a small, well-sheltered beach in a gap between two groups of houses, and although parking in the road above it is not allowed, there are picnic tables beside the beach which have a pleasant view across Greenwich Bay. It seems to be an ideal place to stop to lunch or rest.

To move into Greenwich Cove and reach Goddard Park beach, you'll round Sally Rock Point, but for almost a nautical mile after you leave Sandy Point behind, Sally Rock Point will not come into view, because it will be eclipsed by a jog in the shoreline. Watch for rocks in the

Fig. 25 *Looking back eastward along the serene shoreline of the south side of Greenwich Bay from the false point east of Sally Rock Point*

water offshore and to the east of this false point and thereafter until you are well around Sally Rock Point.

There's no speed restriction, to my knowledge, on boats in this area, and some powerboats hug Sally Rock Point when entering or leaving Greenwich Cove. You probably should round Sally Rock Point by passing among the rocks there while also being prepared for the arrival of waves from boat wakes. There are always several rocks hardly awash and placed to scratch and dent your boat's hull: It's fun to play among the rocks, but keep your eyes peeled.

The Goddard Park beach begins just after Sally Rock Point and extends along the concave shoreline to Long Point, which marks the entrance to Greenwich Cove. Halfway between is the public beach and parking area; landing and launching are best done toward the Sally Rock (northeast) end of the part of the beach that fronts the parking lot, beyond the area marked for swimming by floats and lines *(fig. 26)*.

Fig. 26 *Goddard Park beach from beyond the swimming area*

Watertrail 2, Launching Site 4: Goddard Park Beach

Goddard Park Beach provides paddlers who want to try the sheltered west end or the south side of Greenwich Bay with essentially unlimited parking, a less exposed location than Sandy Point, and marginally better water quality than Greenwich Cove, where the Goddard Park Ramp is located.

Goddard Park Beach: Driving

Follow signs from Post Road to Goddard Park along Ives Road and enter the park by the main (and usually only open) entrance, then proceed straight ahead. Park near the far end of the lot and bring boats to the water around the far end of the retaining wall and wooden steps.

Goddard Park Beach: Launching

Paddling straight out from shore takes you diagonally across the head of Greenwich Bay into its northwest corner at Apponaug and means spending much of that distance trying to make yourself and your craft seen by all of the considerable numbers of boats passing in and out of the slips and marinas from Greenwich Cove to Apponaug. It is pleasanter, on balance, and safer to paddle left from the beach to Long Point and either enter Greenwich Cove or cross its mouth to the western shore of Greenwich Bay. Paddling to the right from the beaches brings one to Sally Rock Point and the south side of Greenwich Bay.

Watertrail 2, Link 4: Goddard Park Beach to Goddard Park Ramp

Paddle straight out from the beach until you are past the marked swimming area, then swing left (south) and make your way to Long Point. Even if planning to visit the west and north shores of Greenwich Bay without entering Greenwich Cove, paddle to Long Point, because the stream of boat traffic there is narrower and subject to a 5-miles-per-hour limit.

A sandy beach extends around Long Point, which has a sandy shoal extending from its tip; where the beach curves away from the channel on the other side of the point, it becomes a sheltered place where you can pull out your boat, lunch, and rest while watching wildlife in the shade of the wooded bluffs of the narrow cove's east shore and the activity among the workboats and yachts moored in the stream and at slips on the opposite, western shore.

Continue along the eastern shore to the Goddard Park launching ramp.

Watertrail 2, Launching Site 5: Goddard Park Ramp

There's little to recommend the Goddard Park ramp when compared to the Goddard Park beach as a launching spot into the west end of Greenwich Bay, considering its proximity to a crowded harbor and (in warmer weather at least) often dubious water quality.

Goddard Park Ramp: Driving

After entering Goddard Park (see directions to Goddard Park beach), proceed through the checkpoint and take the paved road to the left after the field; a gate at this intersection may close this road to vehicles during late fall, winter, and early spring. Go along this road, keeping to the right-hand paved road at intersections. You will sweep back toward the main road and then turn downhill to the right. At the bottom of the hill, where the paved road turns abruptly left, there's an unpaved driveway into an unpaved parking lot large enough for 30 cars or more. The launching ramp is at the lot's far end.

Goddard Park Ramp: Launching

This launch area offers the benefits of generous parking, a gently sloped ramp and shore, and stable footing on the ramp and ground when launching at middle to high tide. (It's a little squishy at low tide.) Greenwich Cove itself is sedate throughout. The location does, however, have the disadvantage of being on a cul-de-sac a couple of miles removed from the main tidal flow in the West Passage, and this seclusion means that while the water level does rise and fall with the tides, the cove is flushed with barely any oceanic water. Little or no fresh water enters Greenwich Cove from the land, either. The very end of Greenwich Cove, the cul-de-sac itself, seems to appeal to mute swans and assorted smaller waterfowl, and paddlers may enjoy peeking in at them from a distance.

Watertrail 2, Link 5:
Goddard Park Ramp to Apponaug Cove

Cross Greenwich Cove *(fig. 27)* to its western shore anywhere along its length, watching of course for harbor traffic, and make your way past the ends of the mooring slips, past Long Point on the other shore, and out into the southwest corner of Greenwich Bay. Straight ahead is Chepiwanoxet Point, a peninsula that juts out from the middle of the bay's west end, and on its near side stand pilings, perhaps remnants from piers and wharves from years back, abandoned but picturesque even now.

Fig. 27 *West shore of Greenwich Cove is lined with restaurants, workboats, powerboats, and sailing yachts*

Fig. 28 *From Cedar Tree Point at the mouth of Chepiwanoxet Point, Greenwich Cove, and Long Point*

The south side of this small peninsula has steep banks and the end is rocky, but the north side offers enough gaps between the rocks to pull out kayaks and canoes for lunch and rest; it also is a favorite spot of fishermen and at times may be too crowded for you to stop.

Once past the peninsula, continue to the mouth of Apponaug Harbor either by following the shoreline or striking out across the intervening stretch of water on a course of 0 degrees magnetic for a distance of almost exactly 1 NM. This course will bring you to the "green can 3" buoy, but even a small deviation to the east will put a paddler in the channel. Better to shade your course intentionally a few degrees to the west to, say, 355 degrees magnetic, to be sure of staying clear of traffic in the channel entering and leaving the large marina and Apponaug Cove.

Enter Apponaug Cove keeping to the left, where once past the marina there's shallow water clear of moorings. The launching dock and beach are the first you encounter.

Watertrail 2, Launching Site 6: Apponaug Cove Launching Area

Looking at Greenwich Bay as a rectangle 2 NM long (east to west) and 1 NM high, there are launching spots close to all four corners; Apponaug Cove is the one in the northwest, providing a base for paddling along the north side of Greenwich Bay and also the west end, although it remains to be seen what impact marina construction will have on paddling there.

Apponaug Cove Launching Area: Driving

In Warwick on Post Road south of RI 117 and Apponaug center, take Arnold's Neck Road east along the south shore of an inlet visible from Post Road. Follow the road beneath the railroad bridge, bear left where the road divides so as to stay close to the water and drive to the last or next to last parking lot on the left.

Apponaug Cove: Launching

When the tide is more than half full, there's enough depth of water to allow exploring the head of Apponaug Cove on the other side of the

Fig. 29 *View toward the channel that leads to the entrance of Apponaug Cove*

railroad bridge, and the main part of the cove itself offers pleasant, sheltered paddling at any tide. This cove makes a good starting point for trips in either direction along this watertrail, with the only particular preparation being to take advantage of the quiet in the cove to maneuver to the appropriate side of the channel before exiting in front of the marina: move to the east side (shore opposite from launch area) if continuing east along the north shore of Greenwich Bay or to the west side (by the slips) if going south along the bay's western end *(fig. 29)*.

Paddling south from the mouth of Apponaug Cove offers an object lesson in piloting. The skyline is featureless. Where have the yachts, restaurants, and marinas gone? Where on the skyline is the entrance to Greenwich Cove? Chepiwanoxet Point eclipses both and merges with Goddard Park over on the far shore, making it difficult to choose an aiming point with certainty. By following the shoreline you must eventually come to the point and then Greenwich Cove, but if you want to cut off some distance, then the best plan is to have a compass on your boat and a chart or perhaps just a small (waterproofed) reminder sheet with compass headings for the legs of your trip written down. Here, for instance, you would paddle due south (180 degrees magnetic) to find the end of the peninsula and beyond that the entrance to Greenwich Cove. Consider how easily you might have paddled a mile or two out of your way and how difficult it would be to maintain a constant heading in fog, for example, and you'll appreciate that a compass brings safety out of all proportion to its cost. No batteries or satellites are ever required, either.

Watertrail 2, Link 6:
Apponaug Cove to Brush Neck

Paddle east across Apponaug Cove and follow that shore to the cove's entrance, round the sandy spit called Cedar Tree Point, and continue east parallel to the shore until an opening to another cove appears. Enter there and turn through at more than a right angle; you'll see the beach at the end of Brush Neck in front of you. Land toward the left end of the beach; the parking lot is perhaps 50 yards inshore through a grove of trees. You have reached the north end of Watertrail 2.

Cedar Tree Point makes a fine spot to rest and appreciate the panoramic view from Warwick Neck to Sandy Point to Sally Rock Point to Chepiwanoxet Point and around behind you to the buildings and boats of Apponaug. It is also most likely private land above the high tide line, but if paddlers are quiet and spotless then probably they will be tolerated here for some time to come.

Watch for rocks and pilings in toward the shore all along this leg of the trip *(fig. 30)*. You also may be surprised to find your paddle hitting

Fig. 30 *Paddling east along the north shore of Greenwich Bay, nearing the entrance to Buttonwoods and Brush Neck Coves*

the bottom in places, and your boat may even run aground, but just back up or rock yourself loose and try again. No harm done.

There's normally a lot of wildlife to watch, even if none of it is at all uncommon. My favorites are the brants, sociable small dark-fronted geese which move about the upper bay in groups of a dozen or so birds, feeding on sea lettuce and other things brought within their reach in the water churned up from the bottom in the zone where the waves break. Perhaps you'll also see a local specialty, the urban stumpy-legged sandpiper: actually, they're just pigeons, but it is amusing to watch them standing befuddled along the line where dry sand turns to wet, trying to figure out what to do at the beach.

The distance from Cedar Tree Point to Buttonwoods Cove is 1.8 NM, near enough, and sudden rough weather or some other emergency might make you want to land, yet walls and riprap protect most of this shoreline. Rather than risk your boat and yourself trying to come ashore against something sharp and hard, go on (or turn back) until you reach any of the several ramps, small beaches, and other breaks in the protective reinforcement along this stretch.

The inlets to either side of Brush Neck are well worth exploring; Buttonwoods Cove is to the left as you enter from the bay, and Brush Neck Cove, almost twice as long, is to the right.

Watertrail 2, Launching Site 7: Brush Neck

Paddlers who are used to using launching spots in the Oakland Beach section of Warwick ought to consider using Brush Neck instead, as it offers almost total freedom from boat traffic, no tricky currents, plus two long calm inlets to explore, and quick access to the north side of Greenwich Bay.

Brush Neck: Driving

Drive east through Apponaug on RI 117 and after passing beneath a railroad bridge bear right onto Long Street. Follow this road to Buttonwoods Avenue and then across, where its name changes to Asylum

Street. Proceed to the end of this street and enter Warwick City Park. Continue straight ahead on the twisting paved road through the park (speed bumps and bike path crossings!) until you have an opportunity to turn left before reaching practice and ball fields. Follow signs to "Beach" and its parking lot. When leaving, continue along the same road, which will loop around to rejoin the beach access road and then lead you back to the fields.

You'll be moving your boat along the right end of the grove of trees between the parking lot and the water.

Brush Neck: Launching

The coves along both sides of Brush Neck (Buttonwoods Cove to the southwest, and Brush Neck Cove to the northeast) offer about 1 NM of sheltered paddling and some pretty views, but the true utility of Brush Neck is as an entry into the northeast part of Greenwich Bay safe from congested boat traffic and potentially tricky waves and currents. Oakland Beach may also offer access to these waters, but for small boat paddlers the Brush Neck site seems preferable because of its relaxed, secluded atmosphere.

Paddling for relaxation is not suggested to the east of Brush Neck beyond Oakland Beach and along the south side and a short way up the east side of Warwick Neck for very much the same reasons that paddling around Quonset Point was not recommended either: There's a heavily traversed channel from Oakland Beach to Warwick Point and a steep rocky cliff on the south side of Warwick Neck which reflects waves arriving from farther south in the West Passage to create a nearly constant irregular chop at the best of times. Because of the low but rocky cliffs, there are few places to land. Paddling in the corridor among submerged and exposed rocks toward land and boats passing full tilt in the channel is perfectly possible, but it involves more risk and less peace of mind than one looks for in a watertrail. Strong currents along the south face of Warwick Neck must be anticipated as well: The bottom has been scoured out to depths of more than 40 feet; compare that with an average depth about 1/10 of that in the area from Sandy Point to halfway across Greenwich Bay in the direction of Warwick Neck.

Watertrail 2, Loop 2: Brush Neck to Brush Neck Cove, Buttonwoods Cove, and Return

The waters here are so moderate and well sheltered that families trying out paddling might want to come here for the first few times. Probably the principal factor in paddling here is the tide: At low tide your boat may not float. Explore both sides of Brush Neck; as you stand on the beach, Buttonwoods Cove is to your right and Brush Neck Cove is back around the point to your left *(fig. 31)*.

Fig. 31 *Still waters and quiet docks in Brush Neck Cove*

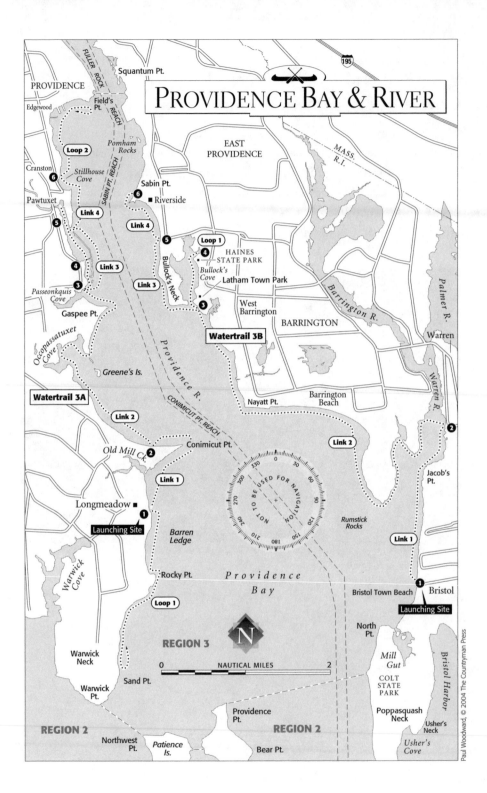

PROVIDENCE BAY & RIVER

195

Squantum Pt.

PROVIDENCE

Edgewood

Field's Pt.

EAST PROVIDENCE

FULLER ROCK REACH

Loop 2

Pomham Rocks

Cranston

Stillhouse Cove

6

Pawtuxet

SABIN PT. REACH

Sabin Pt.

6

Riverside

MASS. R.I.

Link 4

Link 4

Loop 1

5

Link 4

5

4

HAINES STATE PARK

Palmer R.

Link 3

Bullock's Neck

Bullock's Cove

Latham Town Park

4

Link 3

3

3

West Barrington

Passeonkquis Cove

Barrington R.

3

BARRINGTON

Gaspee Pt.

Warren

Occopassatuxet Cove

Watertrail 3B

Providence R.

Greene's Is.

Warren R.

Watertrail 3A

Nayatt Pt.

Barrington Beach

Link 2

CONIMICUT PT. REACH

Link 2

2

Old Mill Ck.

2

Conimicut Pt.

Jacob's Pt.

Link 1

330   0   30

NOT TO BE USED FOR NAVIGATION

300   60

Longmeadow

1

270   90

Rumstick Rocks

Link 1

240   120

Barren Ledge

210   180   150

1

Warwick Cove

Rocky Pt.

Providence Bay

Bristol Town Beach   Bristol

Launching Site

Loop 1

North Pt.

REGION 3

N

Mill Gut

Warwick Neck

0   NAUTICAL MILES   2

COLT STATE PARK

Bristol Harbor

Sand Pt.

Poppasquash Neck

Warwick Pt.

Usher's Neck

REGION 2

Providence Pt.

REGION 2

Usher's Cove

Northwest Pt.

Patience Is.

Bear Pt.

Paul Woodward, © 2004 The Countryman Press

Watertrail 3A: Providence Bay and the West Shore of the Providence River, from Sand Point to Field's Point

*T*HIS WATERTRAIL goes past some of the most heavily populated areas in Rhode Island and is the most easily reached from Providence, Cranston, and Pawtucket. It makes use of a continuous north-south corridor for relaxing kayaking and canoeing that stretches 7 NM from Sand Point near the tip of Warwick Neck to Field's Point in the north at the city border between Cranston and Providence.

Paddlers along this watertrail move through a spectrum of paddling conditions, from the waves out of the Upper West Passage that reach Sand Point along Warwick Neck to the relative calm along the northerly links of the route.

Watertrail 3A uses 5 launching sites: Longmeadow, Conimicut Point, and Passeonkquis, Pawtuxet, and Stillhouse Coves. There are other places to launch along the route, but for various reasons these other sites are less attractive for paddlers and are considered secondary: George B. Salter Memorial Grove and the Pawtuxet Harbor launching ramp, for example.

Two points without launching access but with a sandy beach make pleasant destinations: Rocky Point south of Longmeadow and Gaspee Point between Conimicut Point and Passeonkquis Cove. Also, parallel to the shore at the George B. Salter Memorial Grove is a long, large rock breakwater connected to the land by a low causeway; the sheltered waters behind the breakwater both north and south of the causeway make good paddling playgrounds. You can also pull ashore and lunch either at the causeway or on the low grassy dots of land at the south end of the breakwater (Rock Island).

Watertrail 3A, Launching Site 1: Longmeadow Boat Ramp

Longmeadow is situated on the west shore of the West Passage, still in Warwick but well up toward Cranston and Providence, north of Rocky Point and south of Conimicut Point. There's actually little to sway one in choosing between this launching location and the beach on the south side of Conimicut Point, but Longmeadow is almost invariably less crowded and not encumbered with lines of surfcasters fishing from the beach. Longmeadow has a boat-launching ramp of concrete crossties edged by flat, slippery rocks, whereas Conimucut Point has gently sloping sand.

Longmeadow Boat Ramp: Driving

West of the curve in RI 117 (West Shore Road) where it bends to the north, Warwick Neck Road branches off to the south. Follow it until an enclosed salt pond appears on the right and turn left up a small rise onto Samuel Gorton Road. Follow Samuel Gorton Road to its end in a public launching area. The parking area often has large puddles of opaque, silty water, and these can be quite deep and conceal sharp objects, so consider probing these puddles before driving or walking through them.

If you're interested in birds and find you're alone, consider approaching the beach quietly. You could find a flock of brants, numerous killdeer, semipalmated plovers, black-bellied plovers, and others. Look along the shore north of the ramp, too.

Longmeadow Boat Ramp: Launching

An old launching ramp is to the left, in front of the north end of the parking area, and is usually the best place to launch and land. Be careful of your footing on the concrete and stones when the tide is low. The bottom is generally stony in front of Longmeadow and remains the same depth until some distance from shore.

The 1-fathom line lies about 350 yards directly offshore at Longmeadow and draws closer to the shore as one goes south. On the shore side of a line from Longmeadow to the sandbar at the tip of Conimicut Point the water is shallow and typically sedate, making this cove at the mouth of Old Mill Creek an inviting place to practice and transition from flat water to saltwater.

South of Longmeadow and north of Rocky Point the bottom is rough and rocky, and if you look in the direction of about 150 to 155 degrees magnetic you may be able to pick out Barren Ledge, beloved of cormorants and exposed most of the time. It sits 400 yards from shore and marks where the 1-fathom line begins to swing closer to shore.

Directly east across the bay from Longmeadow is Rumstick Rock, off the end of Rumstick Point, and then, about 3.4 NM across the water from Longmeadow, the shoreline of the town of Bristol; from this angle, the town of Warren is tucked in behind Rumstick Neck. Boat traffic between the channel at the level of Conimicut Point and the strait between Warwick Point and Patience Island usually travels more than 0.5 NM offshore from Longmeadow. For the remainder of the distance, however, expect fast north-south boat traffic until you are near the opposite shore.

The waters at Longmeadow are most exposed to winds from the east-northeast through south-southeast; with the latter wind, waves can roll in from the East Passage across a fetch of about 6.5 NM.

Watertrail 3A, Loop 1:
Longmeadow South along Warwick Neck
Past Rocky Point to Sand Point and Return

Launch from Longmeadow, gain about 50 to 100 yards offshore, and head south along the shore, which is faced with stone, timbers, and small, steep beaches where one may hear and catch sight of killdeer, a medium-sized plover that is more associated with our vanishing pas-

Fig. 32 *Placid water by Highland Beach on the north side, on this day the lee, of Rocky Point*

tures and meadows than the beach. After paddling south 0.65 NM, the shoreline sweeps out abruptly to form Rocky Point, which although tipped with boulders and bedrock, has a most attractive curved, sheltered beach, Highland Beach, on this northern side *(fig. 32)*.

Fig. 33 *Rocky Point*

Behind the beach lies a wet area with wild roses and large willows, and out toward the point, beyond the end of the beach, lies a tiny, perfect garden of trees, grass, rocks, and water, a little gem that sits against all probability in front of a neglected amusement center in plain view. You might see if you can bag any litter you notice here, just to keep up standards *(fig. 33)*.

If the wind is no more than a gentle breeze, consider nosing around to the bay side of Rocky Point and enjoying the expanding view to the south. Out from this face of the point stands the old Rocky Point pier: Go well around the end of the pier, not underneath it, because unlike many piers this one is built above a rock jetty *(fig. 34)*.

Fig. 34 *Looking back north at the Pier at Rocky Point; don't try to go beneath it!*

Soon after the pier the shoreline recedes back to the west to form the shoulder at the relatively narrow base of Warwick Neck; follow along parallel with the shoreline here so as to stay in shallow water and shoreward of boat traffic. Watch for submerged boulders in this bight; there are only a few, but somehow they're like light poles in a parking lot, always getting in the way *(fig. 35)*.

As the shoreline bends southward again, along Warwick Neck, stone buildings, one decrepit, another in good repair, stand along the shore. Shellfisherman gather and disperse in the angle formed by the

Fig. 35 *Out of Rocky Point's lee, looking south along the side of Warwick Neck*

Fig. 36 *Approaching the pier at the end of Sand Point toward the end of Warwick*

north ends of Patience and Prudence, and both pleasure and work boats straighten out and take aim for the narrow passage at Warwick Point a mile farther on.

Continue south in front of the vast sloping green lawn that appears next and proceed beyond this, if you wish, but for moderate paddling it is better to turn around in the neighborhood of Sand Point (which is not the same as Sandy Point across the mouth of Greenwich Bay from Warwick Neck and is a launching site included in Watertrail 2). Just 0.25 NM beyond Sand Point current, tricky waves, rocks, and traffic start to combine and increase the number of factors impinging upon a paddler intent on rounding the south end of Warwick Neck *(fig. 36)*.

Watertrail 3A, Link 1:
Longmeadow to Conimicut Point

As mentioned above, the waters shoreward of a line from Longmeadow to the sandbar off the top of Conimicut Point are shallow and usually gentle, so a paddler can easily go north from Longmeadow more or less along the shore toward Conimicut and typically have a pleasant, relaxing ride of about a mile: 0.5 NM to the base of the point and 0.5 NM out along the point, being possibly obliged to swing wide of the beach in the neighborhood of the point itself because of fishermen using surf-casting gear. The issue of fishermen arises all over Conimicut, even on the wave-washed sandbar at the tip; just watch for lines and hooks.

People line both sides and the tip of Conimicut Point, even standing out on the long submerged sandbar that extends from its tip. Others sit and watch, lie back in the sun, or walk across the lawn of the little park.

Just after low tide, when the sandbar that forms the wispy end of Conimicut Point has been covered by the flooding tide to a depth of only a few inches, gulls stand up to their knobby knees in the shallows, facing south, alert to snap up whatever tidbits the current sweeps their way. South of the bar, terns patrol from the air and plunge for minnows.

Launching and landing can be done on both the north and south sides of Conimicut Point, but the dedicated launching area is on the north side, meaning that the paddler approaching from the south must round the point. This can be done quite reliably about a third of the distance from the land at the tip of Conimicut to the lighthouse.

Fig. 37 *Launch site on the north side of Conimicut Point seen from the water*

The north side launch site is just before the first house and after a small jetty of rocks *(fig. 37)*.

Watertrail 3A, Launching Site 2: Conimicut Point

Conimicut Point is another of the narrow, long, and sandy barriers that thrust out into the Providence River and the upper bay: One may wonder what keeps these from washing away or shifting like a dune, yet on Blaskowitz's map of Narragansett Bay in 1777, you'll find Conimicut in the same place as today, with the same shape and the same name.

Given the propensity of winds to blow up the bay from the south, Conimicut creates over a square mile of semicircular lagoon in its lee, a treasure for paddlers or rowers seeking clean, calm water.

Conimicut Point: Driving

RI 117 on the east side of US 1 in Warwick has the unlikely shape of a "sleeping-U," with its open end to the west and its bottom to the east, where it is called West Shore Road. Where it reaches farthest east, side roads with names like Symonds, Waverly, and Stokes branch off to the east. Follow any of these to reach Shawomet, which parallels the north shore of Conimicut Point, and follow it to its end, always choosing to stay close to the north shore; another road out along Conimicut Point a short distance to the south enters the park at the point, from which it is marginally less easy to launch.

Although the surface of the parking area at the end is loose and highly uneven, there is space for half a dozen vehicles at least, but be aware that boat trailers have to be maneuvered in and out of the water at the section of beach immediately beside the lot and for that reason the middle of the lot and its north (water) end must not be blocked.

Conimicut Point: Launching

The main caution to sound regarding Conimicut Point is not to venture beyond the lighthouse except with good reason *(see fig. 38)*. Do not

Fig. 38 *From launch site out along Conimicut; note the heavy shipping*

go even that far from the point but stay within half the distance to the lighthouse from shore.

Paddling south from Conimicut, stay shoreward of a line from the point to Longmeadow or Rocky Point.

Traveling north, stay shoreward of a line from the launching site to the base of Gaspee Point, visible as a bright sandy beach upriver on the same side, and even that is cutting the margin of safety quite fine; the dangerous factor in this case is the path of the shipping channel, which turns from almost northwest in the Rumstick Neck Reach south of Conimicut Light to nearly west-northwest in the Conimicut Point Reach, only deflecting to north-northwest (approximately) at a point on a line connecting Conimicut Point and Gaspee Point. Safer is to head no closer to north than 310 degrees magnetic for at least 1.0 NM after rounding Conimicut Point; from the north-side launching site, up to 335 degrees magnetic is probably safe. Best, of course, is to follow the shore.

Seen from Gaspee Point, the situation is easier to describe: Any position west of a line due south magnetic from Gaspee Point is safely away from the shipping lane; conversely, if Gaspee Point is at a bearing from your boat greater than 0 degrees magnetic, that is, if it is to your east (magnetic), your position is good.

A new factor has emerged that affects paddlers in Region 3, particularly north of Conimicut Point: the high-speed ferry "Ocean State" hurtles between Providence and Newport. Aside from the additional risk it brings to crossing the channel as an instance of heavy, fast-moving traffic, it imposes a risk at a distance as well, as it generates a wake that consists of three to six slow, steep, closely spaced waves that can still be breaking continuously as much as 0.3 NM from its path. The waves are capable of upsetting a kayak with little stability, whose paddler may need to brace directly into the face or back of one of these wake waves to stay upright. One ought to keep an eye out for this ferry, which has the proportions of a shoebox with a chisel nose; anticipate that at some time after it passes through "your" section of the bay you'll be affected by its wake, keep watch for the wake's arrival, and prepare.

Watertrail 3A, Link 2: Conimicut Point to Passeonkquis Cove

Link 2 of Watertrail 3A often combines the best features of both the south and north parts of the upper bay, the cleanliness in the south and the shelter in the north, and adds special attractions of its own, the mouth of Occupassatuxet Cove and the beaches of Gaspee Point. While following the shoreline north from the Conimicut Point launching area you'll also pass houses and gardens, which, in season, revel in colorful

Fig. 39 *Flowerbeds and houses where the Conimicut neighborhood faces the Providence River*

decorations and blooms *(fig. 39)*. Where the houses draw back from the shore, on the south side of Occupassatuxet Cove's entrance, tidy piers (one painted pink!) extend out over the salt marsh grass *(fig. 40)*.

As far as natural beauty goes, Occupassatuxet Cove at high tide in low afternoon light may be the loveliest spot in the bay. It is jammed with shy wildlife, so please enter and proceed with reverence, for here once more is the tension between appreciating and disturbing nature. It is better not to go in beyond where the waterway starts to narrow. This is possibly the best and most precious and productive breeding ground left in Region 3 of the bay system, and even paddlers, the least disruptive of watercraft users, can feel satisfaction at leaving such a jewel undisturbed. There's nothing that our presence can do to help it; it is fine on its own.

Another place to stay away from is the little sandbar called Greene's Island that lies off the mouth of Occupassatuxet Cove; it appears to be a nesting site and feeding ground for least terns and other species even more sensitive and human-averse, such as American oystercatchers. Stop at Gaspee Point instead. Swing out around the northern side of Occupassatuset Cove's entrance and slide out along the south side of Gaspee Point to its tip. There's hardly a better spot to stop for rest and refresh-

Fig. 40 *Toward Occupassatuxet Cove*

ment than Gaspee Point along this watertrail. It is the last undeveloped point of land in this part of Narragansett Bay, the lingering guest, the last trace of what was: When it goes, we shall have built a locked room filled entirely and only with what we ourselves have made. Treasure Gaspee Point.

The launching site at Passeonkquis Cove is easily found from Gaspee Point; it lies in from the houses on the next point of land and out from the cove itself, specifically, just on the bay side of a rocky outcrop. There's a hardened ramp available, or one can land where there are gaps in the grass just as conveniently.

Watertrail 3A, Launching Site 3: Passeonkquis Cove Ramp and Beach

It's easy to understand why some paddlers who know about Passeonkquis Cove don't find any reason to launch their kayaks anywhere else. One immediately enters an area with good water quality and reliably mild conditions and can visit Gaspee Point in minutes or proceed down to Conimicut for a longer trip. As it is practically beside the southern opening of the placid waters behind the Salter Grove barrier, even beginners can find a quiet place to practice.

Passeonkquis Cove Ramp and Beach: Driving

RI 117 is made to perform more duties than the average route. After making the "sleeping-U" through Warwick east of the airport—where the legs of the "U" are connected north-to-south by RI 117A, also "Warwick Avenue"—RI 117 turns north to pick up where RI 117A left off (while keeping the name "Warwick Avenue"). 1.6 miles north of the intersection where this occurs is an intersection with a traffic signal where Narragansett Avenue, another of the ubiquitous "Narragansett" streets, roads, avenues, and lanes around the bay, goes east. Now, this Narragansett is also asked to perform extra duty, because first it goes east until nearly at the water and then turns north, even a little west of north, which gives it the shape of a "reflected-L."

Drive east along the lower leg of this "L" and immediately after the angle where you begin to ascend the north-pointing leg, look for a chance to turn right: There are two. These short side roads meet a north-south street even closer to the water than Narragansett Boulevard was with the slightly inaccurate name of Gaspee Point Drive. Follow it south to its end at the Passeonkquis Cove Public Ramp *(fig. 41)*.

Fig. 41 *Launch site at the north side of the mouth of Passeonkquis Cove*

There's parking for perhaps eight vehicles in the unpaved lot and a pleasant little launching beach at the middle front of the lot, plus a hardened ramp to the left as you face the water.

Passeonkquis Cove Ramp and Beach: Launching

Canoeists and kayakers will be pleased to learn that this site has adequate parking, both a ramp and some sandy/muddy surfaces *(fig. 42)*, and a location that places the paddler right astride a 400-yard-wide (0.2 NM) corridor of fairly well-sheltered waters free at most times from fast boats or "watercraft" (that is, a Jet Ski). The shipping channel stays parallel to this shore, so one can count on ship and boat traffic maintaining their distance. Just north of the launching site, around the small nose of land, a long rock breakwater parallels the shore and is attached at about its midpoint to the mainland by a raised pathway that blocks a

Fig. 42 Kayaks launching into Passeonkquis Cove close to low tide

paddler unwilling to portage from traveling inshore of the breakwater from end to end. The channel side of the breakwater may look steep and forbidding, but there seem to be no submerged boulders along that margin to endanger small craft, so one can safely paddle alongside the breakwater provided one keeps a reasonable separation distance. Attempt landings either at the southern end, where there are low-lying islets (Rock Island), or along the northern arm on ground exposed around low tide, particularly on the landward side.

A drawback of the area, though, is that the bay's water rapidly becomes turbid, typically, north of Passeonkquis Cove.

Watertrail 3A, Link 3: Passeonkquis Cove to Aspray Boathouse, with George B. Salter Memorial Grove

To reach the Aspray Boathouse in Pawtuxet Village, you must choose how to deal with the 0.45-NM-long breakwater *(fig. 43)* that lies off-shore and parallel to the route between the two. Venture inshore of the barrier and portage across the narrow isthmus connecting the barrier to the mainland or paddle offshore of the barrier and deal with currents and boat traffic not so much alongside the breakwater as at the entrance

Fig. 43 *From well out along the northern arm of the barrier off Salter Grove*

to Pawtuxet Harbor. A family outing with children might opt for the former, keeping close to the shore and treating the short portage as a small adventure.

Boats moor inshore of the barrier's northern arm and Pawtuxet Neck, and behind Pawtuxet Neck, large powerboats tend to hug the shore of the neck where the water is deeper, so paddlers must avoid finding themselves squeezed against pilings by using the landward side of the waterway.

At the north end of the barrier is the mouth of the Pawtuxet Harbor (*fig. 44*), which extends behind the land in the right-hand side

Fig. 44 *View northwest toward the mouth of Pawtuxet Harbor*

of the accompanying picture. Be on high alert at this intersection. Boat traffic here must be carefully watched, as it is entering and leaving from left and right both in front and behind, as well as toward and away from the viewer; it has the form of a capital "H" with the uprights running north-south, the left-hand upright behind the barrier and up into Pawtuxet Harbor and the right-hand upright outside the barrier and Pawtuxet Neck.

Watertrail 3A, Launching Site 4: George B. Salter Memorial Grove, North and South

Salter Grove seen from the point of view of a paddler is primarily a place to putter about in very well protected waters, especially south of the isthmus, where the water is especially shallow. Having trouble keeping your boat going in a straight line? Practice here, out of traffic, waves, and (usually) wind.

George B. Salter Memorial Grove: Driving

Follow directions to Passeonkquis Cove, but stay on Narragansett Avenue after it angles north until about 0.7 mi. north of the angle a sign saying GEORGE B. SALTER MEMORIAL GROVE appears on the right, toward the water.

There's ample parking for cars with car-top boats.

George B. Salter Memorial Grove: Launching

Salter Grove provides access to the exceptionally well-sheltered waters behind the 0.45 NM long barrier that parallels the shore between Passeonkquis Cove and Pawtuxet Neck, but due to an isthmus connecting the shore to the barrier the access is to two elongate bodies of water, one opening to the south near the headland of Passeonkquis Cove and the other northward directly toward the entrance into Pawtuxet Harbor behind Pawtuxet Neck. To move between the two requires a short portage across the isthmus.

Launching to the north is marginally easier than launching to the south. There's a clean, gently sloped sand-and-gravel launching area beside the road on the north side of the parking area. To launch to the south, a boat must be brought from the parking lot to the beginning of the isthmus. Portaging across the isthmus is probably easiest at this spot or a little farther toward the barrier.

Watertrail 3A, Launching Site 5: Aspray Boathouse

Aspray Boathouse *(fig. 45)* must approximate closely the Platonic model for the concept of urban canoe and kayak launching facility in parking, aesthetics, and location. Maybe a little more could be done with the masonry so that there would be a firm, slanting surface from which to step dry-footed into your boat at any tide, but that might be gilding the lily.

The only counts against using Aspray Boathouse regularly might be the traffic up and down Pawtuxet Harbor, which it faces, and the fact that the idyllic site at Passeonkquis Cove is so close by.

Fig. 45 *Coming up on the Aspray Boathouse in Pawtuxet Harbor*

Aspray Boathouse: Driving

Follow directions to Passeonkquis Cove, but after Narragansett Avenue angles north, continue for 2.0 mi, where on the right there's a paved entryway that broadens out into a long parking lot with the Aspray Boathouse at the far end, facing Pawtuxet Harbor on the other side.

Scores of kayakers could park and launch from here. The launching area is to the right (south) of the boathouse, sometimes a little muddy but hardly ever inconvenient.

The Aspray Boathouse can be reached more directly from the west, too, as US 1 (here, Post Road), which, farther south, ran along the west side of the T. F. Green Airport, has angled northeast and met RI 117. Continuing on Post Road (no longer US 1) brings you toward Pawtuxet Village. Post Road bears left with an angular bend: Do not follow that, but turn right onto a side street, go two blocks (the side street ends), turn left and go until it ends, and you are facing Narragansett Avenue. Turn left onto Narragansett and the Aspray Boathouse will almost immediately appear on your right.

The Aspray Boathouse can also be reached from the north by coming south along Broad Street, which is named "Narragansett" at the Providence-Cranston line. In Pawtuxet Village, Post Road meets Broad-Narragansett at an acute angle; bear left to stay on Narragansett. After two small side streets on the left, you'll come to the small city park with the Aspray Boathouse, also on the left.

Aspray Boathouse: Launching

The Aspray Boathouse has all the qualities sought in a launching site (aesthetics, parking, easy access to sheltered water) but one: It faces a busy waterway, Pawtuxet Harbor. Stay alert at all times while on the water behind Pawtuxet Neck. Paddlers will surely be tempted to go look at the double-arched bridge over the Pawtuxet River a little farther into the harbor *(fig. 46)*, but they should be aware that the entering river water causes a current that sweeps beneath the boats and floating docks south of the bridge.

The shipping lane is 0.3 NM from the south end of Pawtuxet

Fig. 46 *Farther into Pawtuxet Harbor; the river enters on the left after tumbling down low falls and flows under a bridge*

Neck and moves farther away from the western shoreline until the base of Field's Point is reached, say about at the level of the Edgewood Yacht Club.

Watertrail 3A, Link 4: Aspray Boathouse to Stillhouse Cove Park at Narragansett Blvd. and Windsor Street

Launching from the boathouse ramp keep to the right *(fig. 47)*. The narrow channel can be crowded with boat traffic. Larger yachts have been seen to hug the opposite shore to avoid shallower places closer to the middle of the channel, so paddlers can probably have the easiest time by keeping close along this, the west side of the harbor, both coming and going.

The fastidious paddler may not wish to go north of Pawtuxet Neck as the water quality, however much it may have improved in past years, still gives signs and smells of degrading from here north.

Fig. 47 *Toward the mouth of Pawtuxet Harbor from the Aspray Boathouse*

Not much usually happens on the waters between Pawtuxet Neck and the Rhode Island Yacht Club (RIYC) except for encounters with the large local swan population. More than two hundred mute swans form great, white rafts in this area, providing plentiful though skittish camera subjects.

Any eventfulness typically occurs on either end of this link, when you're trying to enter or leave Pawtuxet Harbor, which almost unavoidably involves crossing a channel at least once or picking your way past the ends of the docks nestled behind the arm of land and construction upon which the RIYC buildings stand.

Once having rounded the RIYC bulwark and gotten a view into Stillhouse Cove behind, the launching site near the intersection of Narragansett Boulevard and Windsor Street will be visible on the inner shore as a gap in the tall marsh grass near where the land begins to curve outwards to half-encircle the mooring basin.

Watertrail 3A, Launching Site 6: Stillhouse Cove Park at Narragansett Boulevard (South End) and Windsor Street

The ramp at Stillhouse Cove Park *(fig. 48)* provides paddlers with convenient access to the west side of the Providence River, if they wish to monitor the state of this urban waterway.

Stillhouse Cove Park at Narragansett Blvd. and Windsor Street: Driving

In Cranston, come south on Broad Street until Pawtuxet State Park appears on the right; Windsor Street will be on the left. Follow Windsor to its intersection with Narragansett Boulevard. The launching area is across Narragansett a short way down on the right. Parking may be found along streets in the neighborhood.

Fig. 48 *From the end of the Rhode Island Yacht Club pier across Stillhouse Cove to the ramp at the intersection of Narragansett Blvd. and Windsor St.*

Alternatively, drive south on Narragansett Boulevard almost to its end. Watch for Stillhouse Cove and the ramp on the left, Windsor Street on the right.

From the west or south, come northeast on Post Road (US 1 until it intersects Warwick Avenue), continue into Pawtuxet Village to join Narragansett Avenue (note: not Narragansett Boulevard). Follow Narragansett north; it changes at once to Broad Street. After Ocean on the right and Rhodes and Lockwood on the left, turn right on Windsor. The rest of the directions are as above.

Stillhouse Cove Park at Narragansett Blvd. and Windsor Street: Launching

Opaque as the water may be between this launching site and Field's Point to the northeast, osprey hunt over these waters, certainly a sign of hope for the campaign for the bay's health.

Be aware that although the shipping lane is almost at the opposite shore, a spur boating channel branches off from the main lane at the transition from the Bullock Point Reach to the Sabin Point Reach, continuing along the heading of the Bullock Point Reach, that is, at about 357 degrees magnetic, slightly west of north, aimed at the sharp northwest corner of this expanse of water, which is beyond the Edgewood Yacht Club and near other large marinas. Locate this channel by the pairs of buoys along it. Do not expect boats traveling this lane to be moving slowly; cross this channel quickly.

Watertrail 3A, Loop 2:
Stillhouse Cove Park to Field's Point

A paddler taking all needed precautions about boat traffic may head north into the angle at the base of Field's Point and then move east along the south side of the point. The effluvia of an urban waterfront mar Field's Point, so its attractions, if any, are slight *(fig. 49)*.

Truly dangerous boat and ship traffic should erase the thought of crossing the Providence River at this point from the mind of any paddler. Do not attempt to connect Watertrails 3A and 3B here *(fig. 50)*.

Fig. 49 *North end of Watertrail 3A at Field's Point, looking into the mouth of Providence Harbor*

Fig. 50 *Avoid mayhem! Don't paddle into the Providence River and Providence Harbor channel*

Watertrail 3B: Bristol Town Beach to Sabin Point

Watertrail 3B, an alongshore equivalent of the East Bay Bike Path, offers 11 NM of excellent paddling with natural and architectural attractions. Its first link from Bristol to Warren is 2.25 NM long and pleasant. The second link, 6.0 NM long, is attractive but long, as there seem to be no practical launching and landing places open to nonresidents of Barrington along its bay shoreline other than at Latham Park near the border with East Providence. The links north of Latham Park and nearby Haines Park are scenic, enjoyable, and have readily manageable lengths: 1.0 NM, then 0.75 NM. Incidentally, when there's a strong wind out of the south, even sailing sloops with Nayatt Point and Barrington Beach to leeward cast anchor and ride it out; paddlers in this area find themselves busy.

Watertrail 3B, Launching Site 1: Bristol Town Beach

Paddlers who plan to launch from the bay side of Bristol may want to be aware of the distinction between "Colt State Park" and "Bristol Town Beach"; the former is on Poppasquash Neck and the latter is at its base, arguably still on Bristol Neck. The west side of Poppasquash is rocky and exposed, while the side of Bristol Neck is considerably more sheltered and offers many places to land in a pinch.

Bristol Town Beach: Driving

RIs 114 and 136 run north-to-south down Bristol Neck, the former to the west of center and the latter nearly down the middle.

Coming from the south across the Mount Hope Bridge, stay on RI 114 through downtown Bristol. About 0.75 mi. north of where RI 114, Hope Street, most closely approaches the water of Bristol Harbor on the left (west), there will be a traffic light and an ornate entranceway with two statues of bulls on the west side.

Coming from the north on RI 136, turn right (west) on Gooding Avenue 1.3 mi. after crossing the Warren-Bristol line, then turn left on RI 114 where Gooding Avenue ends at a traffic light and shopping plazas. If you are already on RI 114, watch for Gooding Avenue on the left, the shopping plazas, and the traffic light. About 0.35 mi. south of Gooding Avenue on RI 114, the ornate entranceway and traffic light appear.

Enter between the two bulls and proceed straight ahead along Asylum Road. Perhaps there's another explanation for the name of this road, but it is interesting to note that when the Narragansett tribe was under attack, the women and children are said to have sequestered themselves on Poppasquash Neck, it being more defensible than Bristol Neck in general and particularly the local center of government on Mount Hope itself. This use as a place of refuge could provide an origin for the name "Poppasquash" itself: the language of the Narragansetts used compound words abundantly, forming them from distinctive components of the base words, so, "Poppasquash" (perhaps originally "papoo" + "squa" + "sh") could come from "child" plus "woman" plus "plural feminine ending" (if I'm reading Roger Williams's book correctly).

The East Bay Bike Path crosses Asylum Road at the bottom of the hill after the cemetery on right: Exercise caution. Do not bear left into Colt State Park proper but continue straight to the Bristol Town Beach. Turn right into the large parking lot at the first opening, immediately after the bicycle and skateboard exercise pen. Cross to the far side of the lot and drive toward the water; it may be most convenient to park in a space to the left toward the end of the lot, as the very end of the lot is a traffic lane, not a parking or unloading area.

Canoes and kayaks can be launched from the north end of the beach, which lies outside the swimming area.

Bristol Town Beach: Launching

Due true west across Providence Bay from Bristol Town Beach is the beach in the hollow south of Rocky Point in Warwick, almost 3.5 NM away. Also, a course of 315 degrees true (330 degrees magnetic), northwest can be extended 6.2 NM over water right into the entrance of Pawtuxet Harbor, so by bay standards Bristol Town Beach looks out onto comparatively open water to the west and northward. The shipping lane connecting the East Passage to the Providence River lies close to this shore, and all vessels entering or leaving Cranston, Providence, Barrington, or Warren from Greenwich Bay, the West Passage, the East Passage, Mount Hope Bay, or Bristol Harbor cross the east-west transect across Providence Bay at this level, so canoeists and kayakers contemplating crossing the bay from here should repeat the Paddler's Reality Check:

> *"I'm the lowest, the slowest, the least visible, and most fragile craft out here."*

Heading alongshore southward brings you past the entrance to Mill Gut, a protected salt pond whose narrow opening is spanned by a bridge for foot and car traffic into the state park's waterfront along the bay side of Poppasquash Neck. Beyond Mill Gut, the shore swings out to the west to North Point, then almost due south along the rocky side of Poppasquash Neck for nearly 2.0 NM, where it doubles back northward into Bristol Harbor for a bit over 2.0 NM before turning south-southeast 2.6 NM to Bristol Point and the Mount Hope Bridge. While Bristol Harbor provides delightful, easy paddling, the route connecting the Town Beach and the harbor does not. The bay side of Poppasquash Neck is rocky and affords few places for emergency landings, the shipping and ferry lane passes 400 yards offshore, and the waters, unlike those at the Town Beach, are fully exposed to winds and waves out of the south, where most of the trouble comes from. Paddlers can easily find themselves in an uncomfortably tight corridor between tonnage and vicious wakes on the one side and an exposed, rocky coast on the other.

Paddling northward from the Bristol Town Beach, on the other hand, brings a ride on clean, clear green water in front of family docks and a wildlife sanctuary and then an entry into the Warren River. Because waves coming north through the East Passage have been blocked by Poppasquash Neck from affecting this shoreline, even when the south wind kicks up, the wave patterns remain relatively simple and unidirectional, and if the conditions become too much to handle, paddlers can beach almost anywhere along the way to wait out the blow.

Watertrail 3B, Link 1: Bristol Town Beach to Warren Town Beach

This first link in Watertrail 3B is 2.1 NM long and introduces the paddler to a pleasant length of shoreline aligned almost due true north from where one often sees vivid "seascapes" with the "vault of heaven" reflecting in a wide expanse of smooth bay water to the west. It is pleasant to stroke with the paddle here, for bubbles entrained into the

Fig. 51 *Bristol Town Beach, looking north from the launch area*

water by the blade turn green at depth then, rising and becoming white, burst within the whirlpool that spins where the blade has left the water and with its dimple are swept behind.

Look for ruddy turnstones between the grass and the beach at Jacob's Point, now an educational center and wildlife sanctuary of the Audubon Society of Rhode Island. Hug Jacob's Point, cross over to the

Fig. 52 *Looking north into Warren River from Jacob's Point*

river shore, and continue north *(fig. 52)*. Several small side streets reach the water here and end in tiny beaches where rowboats may lie askew and right side up, or overturned but ready for use; Warren, it seems, incorporates free access to its river into daily life, and from the looks of the waterfront this access has not been abused.

Pull into the town beach at the southern boundary of the property at a small beach of shells beside a curved knuckle of land reinforced with sloping rocks around its edge.

Watertrail 3B, Launching Site 2: Warren Town Beach

This is an invaluable launching place, because it provides public access to some wonderful shorelines and to harbors and rivers upstream that are not described in this book.

Warren Town Beach: Driving

From the north, come south through Barrington and enter Warren on RI 114. Bear right onto Water Street about 0.25 miles after the bridge. Once on Water Street, drive south (river on your right) to where the main flow of traffic is directed left and a sign announces TOWN BEACH straight ahead.

Alternatively, come south on RI 136 from I-195 and US 6 in Swansea into Warren and take RI 103 west. RI 103 will meet RI 114, Main Street in Warren; either cross over Main Street and proceed to Water Street for a left turn there, or turn left onto Main Street and turn right on Bridge Street, about 0.75 mi. to the south. Turn left at the intersection of Bridge and Water Streets to reach the town beach.

From the south, come north into Warren on RI 114 and look for Bridge Street about 0.8 miles north of the Warren-Bristol border.

Parking is free to residents of Warren with a sticker and currently costs five dollars for nonresidents.

Warren Town Beach: Launching

Walk boats along the south fence of the Warren Town Beach property *(fig. 53)*. There's a gap in the streetside fence at the top of the tree-shaded lawn, and a small beach for launching at the water past the end of the fence. A neighbor's house is only feet away, so quiet is probably appreciated.

Fig. 53 *Warren Town Beach canoe- and kayak-launching area*

Heading alongshore to the south is pleasant and easy; remember, though, that Jacob's Point may be shielding this area from the waves and weather beyond.

Upriver, to the right, boat traffic may be lively; stay on "marina alert."

Across the river is Adam's Neck in Barrington, and Watertrail 3B continues by crossing the Warren River channel here and then heading south along that shore to Adam's Point, Smith's Cove, Rumstick Neck, and Rumstick Point, and then north along the other side of Rumstick Neck toward Barrington Beach.

Fig. 54 *Looking east across the Warren River at sailboats and the shore of Warren south of the town beach*

Be careful crossing the Warren River. Keep the boats bunched, travel quickly, have whistles ready to blow, and never presume you have an enforceable right-of-way. Shipping can appear on the water a minute after a departure whistle blows. Hug the opposite shore once there, too, because beyond the channel sailing classes consisting of 20 youngsters in 10 boats may be swirling pell-mell around their practice course, and they're reacting to their instructor the best they can; they do not have eyes or ears for paddlers *(fig. 54)*. By the way, crossing farther south toward the river mouth puts a paddler in the path of boats not yet subject to the 5-knot speed limit: best cross at the Town Beach.

Watertrail 3B, Link 2: Warren Town Beach to Latham Park or Haines Park

Cross the Warren River at the Town Beach, and hug the opposite shore or at least the ends of the private boat docks along the east side of Adam's Neck until its end at Adam's Point. If you have time to turn right into Smith's Cove, you may find Mr. and Mrs. Osprey and the children at home on their nest platform on the west side of the cove where it narrows, and if you do not frighten them, they may continue their softly whistled domestic discussions; they sound like goldfinches from a distance, but closer you hear that they speak in louder voices, yet ones soft and endearing.

Out along the east side of Rumstick Neck, a narrow opening, which at high tide may be entered by canoe or kayak leads to a "lost world" in-

Fig. 55 *Rumstick Point's "Lost World"; Dutchman's slipper seashells and tufts of pink and white flowers can be seen*

side Rumstick Point *(fig. 55)*. Obscured by labels or simply omitted from most charts, a pristine salt pond hides unseen behind the steep, narrow barrier beach, the facade that Rumstick Point shows passersby. Obviously treasured by nearby residents and a small, delicate habitat, it is another of those very few remaining places around the bay that can be protected but hardly improved by our intervention; nonetheless, a peek around the corner at this nursery and haven quite probably is harmless and surely delightful.

Round Rumstick Point leaving a margin for rocks and shoals near its tip. Stop for a rest on the beach and a spectacular view down the bay. Evaluate the weather situation *(fig. 56)*. Driven before one of the strong south winds that spring up in the afternoons the waves from Rumstick

Fig. 56 *Strong rising south wind scuffs the water just south of Rumstick Point*

Point to Latham Park can turn nasty, as the waters receive waves from both the West and East Passages at about equal strengths. These two wave trains intersect at an angle of about 40 degrees, and the result for a kayaker can be uncomfortable. Then again, slogging upwind off the side of Rumstick Point I met two carefree kids and a dog in a 14-foot canoe coming downwind at a run apparently not caring which direction their bow pointed; they seemed to be enjoying the experience and made their port at last, I assume. (They were not mentioned in the news that evening.)

Public access to this shore seems effectively nonexistent. Unless you are a resident of Barrington and can take your boat out at, say, Barrington Beach, then 3.5 NM of alongshore paddling between Rumstick Point and Latham Park still remains. Presumably in an emergency one could land at the west end of Barrington Beach, where residents may launch small boats, and retrieve your boat to the parking lot; it seems unlikely that a nonresident would be barred if in real need. There's also a public access path down to the beach between Barrington Beach and the Rhode Island Country Club beyond a band of trees toward the Nayatt Point end of the Beach, but parking is not permitted on the streets above the access path, making this supposed facility a fairly meaningless gesture useless to all but a few.

Fortunately, though, it is a lovely paddle along the long southward-facing beach between the base of Rumstick Neck and Nayatt Point; almost 1.2 NM long, this may be the longest sand beach in the bay system, even longer than Narragansett Beach or Second Beach beside Sachuest Point.

Fig. 57 *Feeding time at Nayatt Point*

Mind the rocks off Nayatt Point and, at dead low tide, the shoal just south of them that extends about two-thirds of the way to the boulder farthest from shore. If you do happen to come by on an incoming low tide, swing far enough out to avoid distracting the gulls and even egrets that stand knee- or ankle-deep, respectively, in the swift-flowing shallows, pecking and stabbing at minnows and other dinner dishes being conveyed directly to them. *(fig. 57)*

The converted lighthouse on Nayatt Point *(fig. 58)* with its white coat, square-sectioned tower, and porches can seem to be a vision from the Caribbean when the sky and water are intensely blue.

The marshy shore north of Nayatt Point hosts great blue herons reliably. Then comes an attractive line of older waterfront houses, then Latham Park. Land at the beach just south of the headland at the south side of the entrance to Bullock Cove *(fig. 59)*.

Fig. 58 *Nayatt Point Light seen from the west*

Fig. 59 *Entrance to Bullock Cove, straight in along the approach channel; Latham Park (at right)*

Watertrail 3B, Launching Site 3: Latham Park

Latham Park is the best place to start from when exploring the east shore of the Providence River below Sabin Point *(fig. 60)*. It seems to be a better place than Haines Park to launch from in almost every respect. It is directly on the bay and not buried deep inside a busy, narrow harbor. Not only does this save a little paddling and avoid encounters with harbor traffic, but it enables one to see and feel conditions on the bay while preparing to launch; the Haines Park launching site is so sheltered from wind that one can remain oblivious of the true situation out on the water until at the cove's entrance. Quite often, too, Latham Park smells distinctly better than the rocks around the Haines Ramp.

Fig. 60 *Latham Park's launching beach, in front of low retaining wall*

Latham Park: Driving

One way to reach Latham Park is to go to the west end of Lincoln Avenue in Barrington. Lincoln Avenue's east end is on the south side of Barrington High School, which borders RI 114 (County Road at that location) across from the white Congregational Church beside the Massasoit Avenue bridge over the Barrington River.

The west end of Lincoln Avenue is at Washington Road; just to the north on the other side, Bay Spring Avenue continues west. Follow it to (yet another) Narragansett Avenue. Turn south on Narragansett, go to Latham Avenue (the third cross street), turn right, and follow Latham to the end.

Latham Park: Launching

At Latham Park, to reach the beach one has to descend over a rocky shoulder somewhat more than a yard high; consider bringing along an old blanket or pad to help your boat slide over the smoother rocks rather than have to carry it down while watching your footing. Coming in, you can lift the bow onto the grass from the beach, hold up the stern, and slide the rest of your boat straight onto the grass.

The entrance to Bullock Cove is due east of Gaspee Point, although Bullock Point may block the view, and, looking across the axis of the Providence River, is opposite the entrance to Occupassatuxet Cove. The shipping lane's Bullock Point Reach lies in the middle of the river in this neighborhood, about a half mile away. Although in theory there's a sightline all the way south to Coggeshall Point and Melville on Aquidneck Island, 9.9 NM away, under most conditions the constriction of the river formed by Nayatt and Conimicut Points effectively lets pass only a fraction of the energy carried north by waves through the East and West Passages, making the waters north of Bullock Point conducive to paddling even when the waters to the south may be active enough to demand full attention and skill, and the attenuation of waves out of the south improves as one paddles north toward Sabin Point.

Watertrail 3B, Launching Site 4: Haines Memorial State Park

Haines Park, well inside Bullock Cove, is suitable as a starting point for explorations of Bullock Cove itself and the east shore of the Providence

Fig. 61 *Haines Park boat-ramp complex from the channel in Bullock Cove; it's marked by tall pilings*

River. Paddlers, however, should look at Latham Park before deciding on which of the two launching spots to use *(fig. 61)*.

Haines Memorial State Park: Driving

Follow directions to Latham Park, above, but turn north on Narragansett Avenue instead of south. It will enter the park; then, it will pass an entrance to the park on the left, angle to the right, and intersect the East Bay Bicycle Path all at once. Turn left into the park and then take the first right, which will end in a parking lot and boat ramp at the northern border of the park.

Canoes, kayaks, and dinghies are probably best launched from the shore to the left or right of the large boat-ramp and walkway complex directly in front of the lower parking lot *(fig. 62)*. After getting the boat to the beach, cars can be moved to the upper parking lot to take advantage of whatever shade the trees there may provide.

Fig. 62 *Sunken trail usable for launching at Haines Park*

Haines Memorial State Park: Launching

Aside from powerboat traffic in the busy channel down the middle of the harbor, there are no special considerations in Bullock Cove. Paddlers may poke about in the several inlets inside Bullock Cove, particularly around high tide. Bullock Cove opens to the south; paddle out from the launching area beyond the ends of the long docks to the south (left) of the ramp to see the cove's entrance.

The land surrounding Bullock Cove shelters it well. Even when the south wind has kicked up in the afternoon, inside the cove the water may be flat, making this a place to paddle peacefully throughout a sunny summer day. On the other hand, one has difficulty judging the conditions on the bay from inside the cove, and paddling plans may have to be changed in the face of the evidence outside the harbor.

Watertrail 3B, Link 3: Latham Park to Bullock Neck Beach

This link offers a pleasant short paddle with a few surprising views. Cross briskly across the approach channel outside the mouth of Bullock Cove, then work along the shore out to Bullock Point, where the steep, shelly beach at the tip draws back to reveal the Providence skyline. Farther along, two runs of houses overlooking the water are separated by a tree-grown area, and north of the midpoint of this line of trees is an opening

Fig. 63 *Gap in the trees along the side of Bullock Neck marks where Beach Road comes down from Bullock Point Avenue*

through which a short steep road can be seen; this is the Bullock Neck Beach launching site *(fig. 63)*.

Watertrail 3B, Launching Site 5: Bullock Neck Beach

Bullock Neck Beach is a special launching site not just because it opens out into the middle of the stretch between Bullock Point and Sabin Point, but more because it offers a long length of sandy beach where paddlers can practice launching and landing in small waves without there being many, if any, rocks to stay clear of. When you try to find a long sandy beach with public access on the east side of the Providence River, Providence Bay, and the East Passage, you'll begin to appreciate how unusual Bullock Neck Beach really is.

Bullock Neck Beach: Driving

Follow the instructions to Sabin Point Park (this Watertrail, 3B, Launching Site 6) given below. However, instead of turning right off Bullock Point Avenue onto Shore Road, continue on Bullock Point Avenue for almost 0.8 mi. to Beach Road on the right. Beach Road is small, narrow, and steep; it is almost hidden. Across from it is the larger Crescent View Avenue, which is the through road here. Ahead, Bullock Point Avenue ascends a hill and changes its name to Terrace Avenue.

There's space for several cars with cartop boats to park tight against the sides of Beach Road.

Bullock Neck Beach: Launching

This modest launching site conveniently places the recreational paddler at the midpoint of the long north-south eastern side of a rectangular area of (usually) easy bay water about 1.3 NM long and 350 yards wide. There would hardly be a better place in the upper West Bay to practice beach launching and landing with small waves in a place with the feeling but not the impact of a long, exposed shoreline. Move far enough along the shore, naturally, to let the local fishermen carry on their occupation in peace.

Watertrail 3B, Link 4: Bullock Neck Beach to Sabin Point

A paddler can proceed to Sabin Point by following the shoreline closely and may see birdlife in the grassy area up in the angle formed where the shoreline starts to swing west toward Sabin Point. Sandpipers and other shorebirds may be seen along this stretch of beach, too.

Alternatively, the water off Bullock Neck should be free of power-boat traffic for about 300 yards offshore, so one can also head directly toward Sabin Point along a heading of 314 degrees magnetic.

Another alternative is to head offshore to gain sea room until Sabin Point appears at a bearing of, say, 10 degrees magnetic; as the point's bearing creeps up to 25 degrees magnetic, however, your boat begins to dance uncomfortably close to the shipping lane.

The parking lot at Sabin Point is closest to the north side of the Point, where there are both a launching ramp and little patches of natural shoreline many paddlers will prefer to use *(fig. 64)*. Look out for fishing lines when approaching Sabin Point, particularly on its southern side and watch for the fast ferry's wake between the point and the channel.

Fig. 64 *Sabin Point, approached from the south; the ramp is around the point on the north side*

Watertrail 3B, Launching Site 6: Sabin Point

Sabin Point, the northern end of Watertrail 3B, offers parking for a score of cars and access to typically quiet water.

Sabin Point: Driving

First, get to RI 103, variously named Veterans' Memorial Parkway, Paw-tucket Avenue, Bullock Point Avenue, and Willett Avenue, north to south, in East Providence. If it is called Veterans' Memorial Parkway or Pawtucket Avenue where you are, drive south; if it is called Willett Avenue, drive north, at times west. Where the names collide, RI 103 forms a right triangle with a long leg going north from the right angle turn but with southbound traffic (Bullock Point Avenue), a short leg going east (Willett Avenue; the southbound traffic continues to the east), and the hypotenuse carrying now-northbound traffic going north-northwest. Take the long Bullock Point Avenue leg going south; continue straight onto Bullock Point Road. Angle south-southeast, past small streets on the right with names of presidents (Grant, Adams, Monroe, and so on), then angle south after Maple and Oak streets, take the next street to the right, which comes in at an angle approximately west-southwest and is called Shore Road. Follow Shore Road to the end and go into Sabin Point Park. Keep to the right to find the boat ramp and parking lot.

Sabin Point: Launching

Sabin Point effectively terminates Watertrail 3B in the north. It lies on the other side of the Providence River from Pawtuxet Harbor, and the same remarks about water quality lessening upstream apply equally here. The Pomham Rocks 0.8 NM north may be an attraction, but there's a sunken ship along the way, plus a sewer outfall, and the ship-ping lane approaches to within 250 yards of shore; it would be better to paddle elsewhere. About 500 yards straight out from shore is the ship-ping lane's Sabin Point Reach, so the alongshore waters begin to be squeezed by hectic boat traffic from here to Providence.

Watertrail 4A: Conanicut Island, East Side, from The Dumplings to Conanicut Point

*H*ARBORS ARE supposed to be shields from currents and wind, but such protection varies within a harbor and from one harbor to the next. In Jamestown Harbor, the mooring grounds are usually sheltered from the current and the waves, and paddlers for relaxation need have no concerns for their safety beyond the ordinary precautions. They always should remember, though, that they paddle alongside water of potentially overwhelming depth and power and stay aware of when they near the line.

Despite the heightened risks of paddling the channel in this Region, recreational paddlers starting from Jamestown can leave the harbor along a corridor to the north six-boat lengths wide, say, that offers both safety and scenery and goes for about 6 NM, all the way to the northern tip of the island, Conanicut Point.

Watertrail 4A, once it leaves Jamestown Harbor, hugs the island, traveling inside a strip as relatively thin as the skin on a banana, perhaps even the peel of an apple, if apples were as elongate as Conanicut. The 5-fathom line is less than 200 yards from shore along most of the eastern side north of the bridge, and from the bridge halfway to the northern end the 10-fathom line is about the same distance again offshore. Within 6 boat lengths of the shore, a rule of thumb visually easy to apply, the paddling goes easily and safely under reasonable conditions; barring a gale or worse, or heavy surge from a storm, the path beside the shore stays open at any tide.

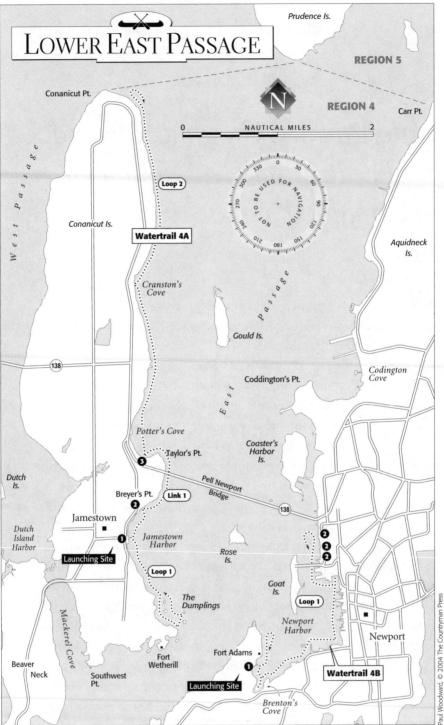

LOWER EAST PASSAGE

Prudence Is.

REGION 5

REGION 4

N

NAUTICAL MILES
0   2

NOT TO BE USED FOR NAVIGATION

Conanicut Pt.

Carr Pt.

Conanicut Is.

Loop 2

Watertrail 4A

Aquidneck Is.

Cranston's Cove

W e s t   P a s s a g e

E a s t   P a s s a g e

Gould Is.

Codington Cove

138

Coddington's Pt.

Potter's Cove

Taylor's Pt.

Coaster's Harbor Is.

3

Dutch Is.

Breyer's Pt.

Link 1

Pell Newport Bridge

138

2

Jamestown

■

1

Jamestown Harbor

Dutch Island Harbor

Rose Is.

2

2

2

Launching Site

Loop 1

Goat Is.

Loop 1

The Dumplings

Newport Harbor

Newport

■

Mackerel Cove

Fort Wetherill

Fort Adams

1

Watertrail 4B

Beaver Neck

Southwest Pt.

Launching Site

Brenton's Cove

Paul Woodward, © 2004 The Countryman Press

Watertrail 4A, Launching Site 1: Jamestown Waterfront, Central

Jamestown Harbor attracts kayakers, as it should, with its many offerings to the visitor onshore and on the water. A persistent problem during the busy season is finding parking, but Jamestown is not large, and parking on side streets away from the water still leaves one merely a pleasant walk to the water *(fig. 65)*. Here's a practical reason for bringing

Fig. 65 *Launching beach in Jamestown Harbor, seen between boats at anchor; use the hotel as a landmark*

a friend paddling and for doubling up the kayaks onto one car: Half the parking spaces are needed, and one of you can stay and watch over the boats and gear while the other parks and walks.

Jamestown Waterfront, Central: Driving

Follow Conanicus Avenue into the business center of Jamestown on the waterfront south of the Pell Newport Bridge and park (perhaps temporarily) in one of the spaces between street and beach north of the pier complex. Carry boats across grass, down over the drop to the beach.

Jamestown Waterfront, Central: Launching

Except for a boat-traffic lane that leads directly out away from the piers to the right of the beach and as long as one stays within the mooring grounds, recreational kayakers should be able to paddle about at leisure.

Watertrail 4A, Launching Site 2: Jamestown Waterfront, North

Less parking than in the center of the waterfront but fewer people using it, too; add in a quiet beach topped by shrubbery and shade, and the north end of Jamestown Harbor might become your favorite local launching spot *(fig. 66)*.

Fig. 66 *Northern launching site in Jamestown Harbor*

Jamestown Waterfront, North: Driving

Follow instructions to Jamestown Harbor waterfront, but at the waterfront's north end, where Conanicus Avenue (if you are coming from the north), comes in sight of the water and the beach, Bayview Drive comes in from the left, making an acute angle with Conanicus. In the "Y" between Conanicus and Bayview stands a large inn. Turn onto Bayview.

Parking spots for vehicles belonging to nonresidents of the local plat can be found a short distance up from the fork on the water side; note the signs posted on the utility poles.

Jamestown Waterfront, North: Launching

There are boat-mooring grounds offshore from the north end of the Jamestown Harbor beach, so kayakers have here as in the center of the waterfront a buffer between them and the main channel *(fig. 67)*. Potter's Cove is up around Bryer's Point and then Taylor's Point to the north (left, facing the water). There's the entire harbor to the south (right) down as

Fig. 67 *Looking south from the northern Jamestown Harbor launch site across the mooring areas*

far as The Dumplings (rocks). Remember that the traffic lane extends out from the main pier. Also, refrain from heading straight toward Bull Point and The Dumplings from this beach *(fig. 66)*, as that route would take one outside the mooring grounds and over the 10-fathom line.

Watertrail 4A, Loop 1: Jamestown Harbor

Slipping away from the beach at Jamestown to wander among the boats at anchor brings a paddler the pleasure of fine scenery, clean water, and close-up looks at boats with character and lovely lines, not all held still at moorings, either: Once, the great thoroughbred 12-meter sloop *Intrepid* hissed across the kayak's bow, then spun upon her heel and cut a flashing wake back out toward Rose Island and the huge suspension bridge to Newport that is the backdrop to every view from Jamestown to the north.

That, by the way, will remind you that there's a traffic lane beginning at the midwaterfront pier that extends outwards from the shore; if there are no moored boats blocking your view of the wharves, and you're looking between a green buoy and a red one, keep paddling, for

Fig. 68 *Man tending his stolid vessel in Jamestown Harbor close to its southern end*

you're in the line of fire. Otherwise, Jamestown Harbor is a fine place to explore *(fig. 68)*.

Down at the southern end are boatyards and the Old Salt Works Beach, and offshore an archipelago in miniature that makes this spot an attraction for sightseers from far beyond Rhode Island. Be ready for some tricky currents there among the islets, though, even near slack tides high or low. In one place the rocks almost encircle you and there's no tugging from the tide, but 20 yards away the current may deflect your boat one way or the other; within the rock garden, however, the nudges will be mild, unlike in the world-class tidal stream just yards beyond the rocks.

Fort Wetherill is around Bull Point to the right only a few hundred yards, but the water beyond Bull Point is far from being a lake; the current there can move at over 1 knot and swirls around the rocks at all times. For combining depth and swiftness, it may be the most extraordinary volume of water in Narragansett Bay. Paddlers looking for an alternate route into Jamestown Harbor from the outside can consider putting in at Potter's Cove and coming into the harbor from the north rather than entering from Fort Wetherill.

Fig. 69 *"The House on the Rock" in The Dumplings; Newport Harbor is directly ahead*

If you are down in The Dumplings *(fig. 69)*, and think of heading north, there's no shame at all in keeping close to shore or at least well in among the mooring area; a course from The Dumplings straight across the mouth of the harbor to the west end of the bridge (or even to Bryer's Point south of the bridge) lies in water that is everywhere more than 70 feet deep and 120 feet deep in places, with a current to match. It is important to keep in mind that the outer limit of Jamestown Harbor is not a line drawn from point to point across its mouth but rather a line that scoops in deeply to almost parallel the shore.

Watertrail 4A, Link 1:
Jamestown Harbor to Potter's Cove

After launching in Jamestown Harbor, stay close to the shoreline and slip between the shore and the bridge's first pier *(fig. 70)*. A group of boats will have to line up single-file. Pay sharp attention to sub-

Fig. 70 *Jamestown Harbor to the north, off Bryer's Point, heading beneath the Pell Bridge*

merged flat rocks from north of the bridge to the turn around Taylor's Point.

Paddle around Taylor's Point and into Potter's Cove; a heading of due west magnetic will bring you alongside the high point of land at the east end of the launching and landing beach, with the parking lot on the first brow on the hill above, an easy walk up.

Watertrail 4A, Launching Site 3: Potter's Cove

Potter's Cove has a lot to recommend it to paddlers. Its location is conveniently close both to popular Jamestown Harbor and to the more natural environs north along the east side of Conanicut. The parking lot is not large, but there are usually open spaces. The cove itself is sheltered and shallow, perhaps even a better place for beginning canoeists and kayakers than the harbor *(fig. 71)*.

Fig. 71 Potter's Cove from the parking area above the cove

Potter's Cove: Driving

Potter's Cove is easy to see; it is the large scoop out of the shoreline immediately to the north of the road on the island side of the tollbooths for the Pell Bridge. Getting to it, however, is harder to describe. From RI 138, once near the bridge take an exit to Jamestown and then look for an opportunity to cross over the opposing lane to a small road that heads up the slope of the hill toward the water, which is Taylor's Point. A short distance up this road on the left is a pullout with room for half a dozen vehicles without trailers. The launching beach lies below the pullout to the left and is reached by a path starting from the pullout's front downhill corner.

Potter's Cove: Launching

Potter's Cove slopes off to deeper water only gradually; 100 yards out from the tide line on the beach the water is still only 2 feet deep and even midway across the mouth of the cove the depth is unlikely to reach 30 feet. Launching from the beach is simple at high tide; at low tide paddlers will have to walk their crafts out through the ooze to get enough water under the keels.

It may be difficult as a member of the general public to get access to the bay north of Potter's Cove. About 1.9 NM north of Potter's Cove, there's an indentation in the shoreline that, on a quite old map, was called Cranston's Cove, but this was at a time when there were only 27 buildings on the island north of Potter's Cove (so says the map). A brook flows into Cranston's Cove, and sandbars have built up there. The water comes close to the roadway, and there's a short path from road to beach. However, there's a NO PARKING ON EITHER SIDE sign posted. There doesn't seem to be even this much chance of getting to the water at the north end of the island, Conanicut Point. Therefore, trips north from Potter's Cove for the general paddler should be planned as roundtrips involving a return to the cove.

It's good to know about the beach in Cranston's Cove; however, it could serve as a haven in an emergency, as well as an emergency take-out point.

Watertrail 4A, Loop 2: Potter's Cove Northward, and Return

Paddle north along Conanicut's shore, staying shoreward of the north-south line of white mooring buoys in Potter's Cove if the wind kicks up. You'll derive a little shelter from the shore and stay away from the cur-

Fig. 72 *Looking south from the north end of Potter's Cove*

rent if the tide is running against you. This will apply if you're coming south along Conanicut and want to continue on to Jamestown south of the bridge, too. If wind, waves, and current are against you, you can evade most of the opposition by turning eastward for Taylor's Point only after reaching the red buoy at the south end of the line of white ones *(fig. 72)*.

Piers puncture the east side of Conanicut; rocks pepper the route, too. A paddler gets good practice reading the ripples and splashes to find the rocks by eye and not by touch, which adds interest to the trip.

Bird life abounds, but of variety there's little: small gulls, middle-sized gulls, and big gulls, plus cormorants. The gulls would be laughing, ring-billed, herring, and great black-backed in September, the cormorants double-crested, with juvenals thrown in.

Fish life abounds. Tens of thousands of 8-inch-long fish dart away from your boat in mid-September; a river of, most likely, herring flows close by the shore from Potter's Point right to the island's northern tip and possibly beyond, although the fish seem most fond of staying over the submerged band of eelgrass beds that lies just off this shore. The fish group themselves by length according to the depth of the water: In 2 feet of water they're 2 to 3 inches long, in 4 feet of water, they're 4 to 6 inches long, and so on. Which raises a question: How does a fish know what kind and size it is itself? A minnow is hardly ever seen to twist around to check the distance to its tail.

The shore itself is mostly rocky. Besides the sandbar at the outlet of

Fig. 73 *A brook flows into Cranston's Cove on the east shore of Conanicut about midway between Potter's Cove and the north end of Conanicut*

the brook in Cranston's Cove, one of the few sand beaches is in the northern angle between the shore and a rock jetty with a gracefully bent and splintered timber protruding from its end. This is 1.0 NM north of the Potter's Cove beach, a little more than halfway to the brook in Cranston's Cove *(fig. 73)*.

Paddlers may find the homogeneous environment along Watertrail 4A from Potter's Cove north to be an agreeable place to build up their range: 1.9 NM from Potter's Cove to the brook, 3.8 NM round-trip, 4.0 NM from Potter's Cove to Conanicut Point, but one cannot stay there, so 6.2 NM, say, with a return to the brook, and 8.0 NM or so for the full trip. In late afternoon the sea breeze may spring up and when returning southward you may find your speed cut by a third or more. Try not to get pressed for time, and carry a strobe flasher for the dark.

The eastern shore of the northern half of Conanicut goes on for several miles entirely uniform in character *(fig. 74)*; a narrow band, less than 100 yards in width, of scattered boulders in the water just offshore, a pier in front of every house or mansion, in front of every pier a boat, and eelgrass under the surface everywhere that sunlight at high tide will reach it and where low tide will still cover it. Beyond this band, the

Fig. 74 *Typical view northward along the eastern shore of Conanicut Island; here, north of Cranston's Cove*

bottom drops off quickly. There are strong tidal currents and a pronounced continuation of whatever is happening in the near-oceanic conditions of the sound as this is still quite far south in the East Passage. The wonder is that the paddling should be so good.

Simply paddle north close to the shore, watching for rocks and slipping through the piers or around them, according to whim. Curve around toward the west at the north end of the island and pull ashore to rest at a beach, half sand, half gravel, east of Conanicut Point, where the inland sea of the middle bay extends for miles uninterrupted, except for Hope Island directly to the north. This view alone can make the trip worthwhile, for land is far away in all directions *(figs. 75, 76)*.

Fig. 75 *Looking east across the north end of Conanicut at the west coast of Aquidneck*

Fig. 76 *Looking north from the north end of Conanicut out over the inland sea*

I have yet to continue around the end of Conanicut and down the west side, but note that unlike the eastern side the deep and powerful channel of the West Passage scrapes past that other shore, and that the current shear will only become worse as you progress to the Jamestown bridges.

Watertrail 4B: Newport Harbor Circumnavigation

WORLD-RENOWNED and much-visited Newport Harbor is one of Rhode Island's main kayaking attractions. It is a lovely place, with many boats and buildings and people to see. A kayaker sees a fresh, entirely different selection of sights around the waterfront than a car passenger or even a pedestrian.

Paddlers who wish to launch their own boats in or near the harbor (not in Jamestown, for example) have sites north and south of the downtown waterfront from which to choose. Paddlers, though, should remember no matter how much Newport Harbor appears to be a playground for small boats, in fact, it was never designed with such craft in mind; nor does it conduct its business so. In the bight between Fort Adams and the Goat Island Bridge are tricky waves, strong currents, fast and busy boats, and surprises hidden potentially behind any of 100 hulls.

Watertrail 4B, Launching Site 1: Fort Adams Beach

With little or no public access for small boats along the downtown waterfront and restrictions on the use of the park on the southern shore of the harbor, the launching spot into the main harbor left to a paddler is in Fort Adams State Park. Fortunately, it is excellent in construction, location, and convenience. About the only conceivable drawback might be that a large group of paddlers' cars might have to split up after unloading, parking some vehicles in the large visitors' lot farther along toward the point.

Fort Adams Beach: Driving

In Newport, drive south on Thames Street almost to the end of the business district; turn right on Harrison Avenue and follow signs to Fort Adams State Park, the entrance to which will be on the right after 1.2 mi. Enter and continue bearing right; at the bottom of a decline turn right onto a small side road to the beach. If you find yourself in the large parking lots for the Museum of Yachting and other attractions, you have driven past the beach turnoff.

Fort Adams Beach: Launching

Kayaks and canoes can be launched conveniently beside the part of the beach reserved for swimmers, beyond a line of floats stretched down the beach and into the water.

The area immediately in front of Fort Adams Beach is sheltered and should be navigable by paddlers of all skill levels, as should Brenton's Cove to the right of the beach. Beyond these areas, however, conditions can be radically different, and novices should be prudent and seek advice before tackling the rest of the harbor.

Watertrail 4B, Launching Site 2: Washington Street Sites

It's useful to know about three launching and landing sites that Newport makes available to out-of-towners and are a short way from the waterfront (about 1.0 NM, almost exactly the same distance as Fort Adams from downtown if you paddle via the harbor's south side, away from the hurly-burly of downtown.

Here, as along the waterfront of Warren but hardly ever elsewhere around the bay, side streets in a residential neighborhood end level with the water, and local families' rowboats crowd in bottoms-up at street- or pathside, making for a sight that seems comfortable and right.

Washington Street Sites: Driving

From the west, cross the Pell Bridge to Newport and take the first exit. Turn right at the bottom of the exit onto RI 238S and right again at the

Fig. 77 *Small launch site in Newport beside Battery Park at Washington and Pine*

traffic signal onto Van Zandt, going west. Continue to the end, then turn left, south onto Washington Street. Watch for side streets on the left with names of trees.

Battery Park, the small park opposite Pine Street, has a small launching beach at the end *(fig. 77)*. (By the way, the battery that used to be in this location is marked on the British Blaskowitz map of 1777.) The two boat ramps are farther on, opposite Elm and Poplar Streets.

Parking on the street for nonresidents' vehicles without trailers is permitted from 6 AM to 6 PM.

From Aquidneck, take RI 114, RI 138, or Coddington Highway to the north end of RI 238 and proceed south to the crossing with Van Zandt, then follow directions above.

Washington Street Sites: Launching

The water in front of Washington Street lies sheltered in the lee of Goat Island and Newport Neck at most times, and the depths out to the distance of Goat Island offshore are no greater than those in Newport Harbor itself. Boat traffic is scanty. Access to the harbor itself may be easier from here than from Fort Adams at times. Just remember that conditions will change beyond Goat Island; a side loop of the East Passage Channel passes east of Rose Island, with depths greater than 50 feet.

Watertrail 4B, Loop 1: Fort Adams Beach to Washington Street, and Return

The route laid out for Watertrail 4B in Newport Harbor is like Watertrail 1B, which circumnavigates Dutch Island Harbor, not just in that both are shielded from the south, open to the west, and partly protected even from that direction by an island, but also in there being in each two well-separated launching and landing spots where paddlers can begin and end a loop around each harbor. Where Newport Harbor differs is in its far greater density of boat traffic, its active waterfront and complexes of piers, the extravagant variety of yachts to be seen, and also, for the paddler, the number of directions from which waves enter the harbor and, once in, recoil from rocks and seawalls all around. Fort Adams will probably be the starting point for most paddlers, so the watertrail description begins there.

Occasionally, interesting boats will be anchored around the curve to the left of the launching beach, offshore from the visitor's center, and a lucky paddler can look closely at historic yachts such as *Courageous* and her cousins *(fig. 78)*.

Brenton's Cove, though, is the next place to investigate, back to the

Fig. 78 *12-meter yachts anchored at Fort Adams Visitor's Center*

Fig. 79 *Entrance to Brenton's Cove beside Fort Adams Beach*

south of the launching beach, a narrowing cliff-sided nook with lovely boats at anchor and seaweed covering the rocks onshore *(fig. 79).*

Coming out of Brenton's Cove, move along the right-hand shore to the breakwater with the Ida Lewis Yacht Club at its end, a handsome sight and a famous landmark. East of Ida Lewis, that is, on the other side of the breakwater, is a sheltered angle where beginning paddlers may choose to spend some time; both here and Brenton's Cove tend to be relatively placid, and if you have rented a kayak to try it out for the first or second time, it might be prudent to wander about in these areas rather than dodge traffic and handle erratic waves nearer the center of the harbor while getting acquainted with your boat.

The Newport waterfront beside Thames Street runs north-south. Paddle north along it to enjoy the sights and activity but treat the waterway between each wharf as if it signaled a busy intersection. If waves in the harbor begin to get the better of you, if you feel precarious in your boat in the chop that sometimes permeates the area, the north end of the waterfront can be a welcome haven, for hardly a strong ripple reaches in past the last few wharves.

Paddle next out to the west in the direction of Goat Island, but keep close to the piers to the north, as yachts, even 12 meters, pass through here on their ways to and from the Thames Street waterfront, and while they might wish to avoid a straying kayak, there may simply be no nearby space on the water large enough to accommodate them in an instant, and they also require time and room to steer and to stop. The Paddler's Reality Check applies in harbors, too.

The structure along whose southern side you are paddling is called Long Wharf or Pier 1; when you come to its end and can look both across to Goat Island and north up along the passage to the low bridge to it, turn north around the end of Pier 1. As you paddle up to the bridge, you may want to look into the slips to starboard, as utterly extraordinary yachts of foreign registry sometimes moor there: sailboats, although that is far too plain a term, with sails that furl by rolling up inside their masts and with tall curved oval windows low on the hull so that looking out to leeward underway would let you gaze slantwise down into the ocean rushing by while to windward you would see the sky.

Fig. 80 *View south toward Goat Island, beyond a thicket of masts*

Continue north and slide beneath the Goat Island Bridge into the area between that bridge and the Pell Bridge *(fig. 80)*. Charming houses, three stories tall but designed and trimmed in such ways that they appear dainty, stand in a row above the banking onshore, and churches and small parks, too. Between the bridges are two public boat ramps that slope into the water at the feet of first Elm then Poplar Streets. North of these look for a small sandy beach beside a rocky shoulder and at the end of a path on the north side of two light-gray dwellings with white trim and tall brick outside chimneys; the beach is in front of a canopy of trees just south of a stone-and-mortar retaining wall with, disappointingly, a plebeian waist-high chain-link fence on top marking

Fig. 81 *Tiny launch site beside Battery Park at Washington and Pine, seen from offshore*

the front of Battery Park *(fig. 81)*. Each location is a possible launching and landing site along Washington Street.

Groups of kayaks sometimes push on to cross beneath the Pell Bridge and go to Coaster's Harbor and Coddington Cove when led by kayakers with local knowledge, but this watertrail turns south here between the two bridges. This area between the bridges is 0.5 NM long, north to south, and is worth exploring for its own sake, as well as being a perfectly good starting point for an excursion into the busier parts of Newport Harbor.

There's an understandable urge to cut some distance off the return trip to Fort Adams by paddling more or less toward the south end of Goat Island and then from there to Fort Adams, but this is not advisable. South of the "green can 3" buoy off the end of Goat Island one encounters just about every vessel of whatever size that is entering or leaving the area. The 5 MPH LIMIT marker is on the waterfront side of the channel here, and powerboats in their eagerness to be on the bay or sound accelerate out from among the boats at anchor. Take the long way back: Go along the waterfront or at least through the mooring areas, and be certain you and everyone in your group know when you are all about to cross a traffic lane.

A paddler, though, should not be put off by these essential precautions from touring Newport Harbor, since if he or she has any feeling for boats at all this is the place to go to see more kinds of craft and greater elegance of line than fill any other harbor in the bay.

Watertrail 5A: Northwest Shore of Aquidneck Island, from Coggeshall's Point to Portsmouth Terminal

THE NORTHERN HALF of the west side of Aquidneck seems to attract no kayakers at all, and yet this is an intensely interesting area, full of history and nature sites. Access to the area is good, too: there are four places in the 4 NM from Carr's Point to Portsmouth Terminal, although only the northern two are covered here. The U.S. Navy Recreational Area at Carr's Point and the Town Boat Ramp just north of that in Weaver's Cove have been omitted.

The two northern sites, Cory's Lane and Willow Lane, open onto waters that give paddlers a view of a region of fascinating geology: an unusually hard coal, *meta-anthracite*, can still be found in outcrops and along the beaches.

The water in this area is even more wonderfully variable than water usually is. On some days it is duck-pond smooth and on other days it rolls about in a delirium as long waves careen up from the south and over from the west. By no stretch of the imagination is this a sheltered mooring ground.

Watertrail 5A, Launching Site 1: Cory's Lane

Cory's Lane provides an entry point into an unusual area that adds a different flavor to the shores beside the bay.

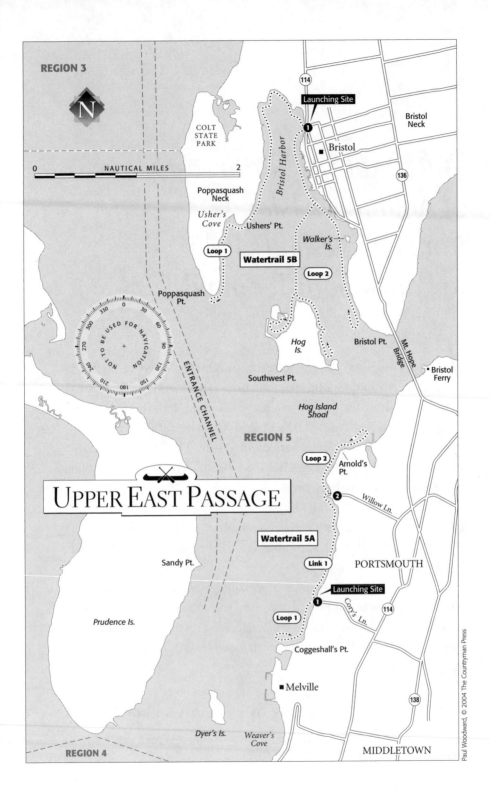

Cory's Lane: Driving

To reach the Cory's Lane launching site when coming from the north, follow directions to Willow Lane launching site, next on this watertrail, but drive 1.3 mi. beyond Willow Lane to Cory's Lane, which is preceded by a sign for the GREEN ANIMALS TOPIARY GARDEN. At the turnoff itself there is a large sign for PORTSMOUTH ABBEY, ST. PHILOMENA SCHOOL, and other institutions. Turn right onto Cory's Lane and drive almost to the end; bear left at the fork in the road toward the topiary gardens, pass the gardens, and park short of (do not cross) the railroad tracks. The paved way beyond the tracks is for foot access and is not to be used for parking.

From the south, come north on RI 114 along the west side of Aquidneck Island and watch for the intersection with traffic light and the road to Melville marina to left. Continue straight, watch for sign announcing GREEN ANIMALS, schools, and abbey, and cross traffic to turn left onto Cory's Lane.

Cory's Lane: Launching

There are days when the sky is blue, the breeze is nil, and only gentle wavelets lend texture to the bay's surface offshore from Cory's Lane between Coggeshall's Point and Arnold's Point, and certainly it must be true that paddling would be peaceful on these days. Then, one could appreciate the gentle tidal current close to this shore, only a third as fast as in the channel along the facing shore of Prudence.

When paddling to write this book, though, I inevitably found waves that took my full attention throughout this embayment, except in the lee of Coggeshall's Point. Not swells, perhaps, but waves with 20 feet between the crests roll in from two directions: up the East Passage and down the long, broad portion of the bay that this site faces, between Prudence and Poppasquash and all the way across the upper bay to Warwick. Now and then a train of waves from somewhere out by Prudence would come in so clear and sharp and steep that I would steal a glance over that way to find the ship or boat that I presumed had generated the wake, but there was none. It just seems to be in the nature of the area to be a magnet for wind-raised waves from anywhere to the west.

Why put this stretch of water in this book at all, then? Because there are times when the water, seen from land at least, does fulfill the promises implied by the scenery, geology, history, and wildlife that crowd this shore.

Watertrail 5A, Loop 1: Cory's Lane to Coggeshall's Point, and Return

As you stand down on the stony beach at Cory's Lane and look 0.5 NM south and 0.6 NM north along the straight shore, you see that the color scheme is black: black rocks, black beach, black outcrops and black earth exposed in the embankment above that—a mile of somber coastline unmatched throughout the bay, to my knowledge *(fig. 82)*.

Begin an exploration of these unusual surroundings by pulling far enough offshore to get your boat clear of the bottom-scuffing rocks and turn south to see the black angle between beach and low eroded cliff that looks dark and cool even on a blue-sky day with sun shining directly into it.

Fig. 82 *Walkway at the end of Cory's Lane*

The rocky beach turns to reddish sand in the crook of the elbow at the base of Coggeshall's Point. This sand must have been brought downhill from the slopes behind by the small but patient brook that empties here.

Turn west along the north side of Coggeshall's Point. The onshore sights change to manmade ones: yachts in cradles, some lacking masts, a dense "To Do" list, a field of bundled reasons why someone's boat is not yet ready for the water.

When you reach the tip of the point, conditions change. Just what they change to depends of course on the tide and the wind. If the tide is low and still ebbing, then the current will be racing south over the sandbar that extends from the point like the ones at Conimicut and Nayatt Points; this one is dotted with boulders, like Nayatt, which raises the stakes of being swept sideways over the bar. If the south wind is blowing strongly, sometimes you can use your paddle as a sail, balance the wind and current's forces, and hang still over the bar to watch fish and birds among the rocks for minutes at a time. At other times it may be easier to swing wide of the point and its boulders and sandbar altogether *(fig. 83)*.

Fig. 83 *Coggeshall's Point, from out of the lee*

This loop of Watertrail 5A, however, turns around at Coggeshall's Point to head back north to Cory's Lane. If your party wants to rest, the coarse sand at the base of the point would be the best place to beach your boats.

The launching and landing spot at the end of Cory's Lane is found by looking for two upright lighter-colored walls above the stones on shore, and an opening with a tarred footpath coming down between the bushes on its northern side. The stones are generally round and smooth and close enough together to make the beach seem cobbled; the footing in the shallows is usually good, so one may enter or leave the boat while it is afloat and held away from larger, sharper rocks.

Fragility

As I was moving back into the lee of Coggeshall's Point midafternoon one day when it was overcast and rainy, two plump-bodied birds with sharp-tipped wings that were set far back on the body, just in front of a short round tail with no legs or feet trailing, swept in paired descending arcs down onto that beach. They might have been small ducks, seen from a distance through eyeglasses blurred by the rain. The wind was blowing past the boat towards them; paddle blades make small, discreet sails, so I let the wind blow my kayak closer to the birds. Fifty yards from them or more, their bills and legs were seen, all orange-red, but then they spooked. Three birds, not two, took off and flew by between the boat and shore: petulant, disdainful American oystercatchers *(fig. 84)*, which even under dull and soggy weather could not find a place to talk and eat away from people. They seemed to blow on instruments, complaining like small boys with plastic whistles, unbirdlike sounds, derisive

Fig. 84 *American oystercatchers abandoning the lee at Coggeshall's Point*

scolding toots from across the water out past Coggeshall's Point. Dyer's Island is over there and then Prudence's south end.

Two seasons earlier, oystercatchers had fled along the side of Hope Island before my kayak could round the island's northern tip. Poor things. The truth? They cannot stand us. Their range is spreading north, maybe in desperation as we occupy the nooks along the coast. They seem to disregard loud engines at a distance, although these must offend them. One hears that different tribes of oystercatchers pass on different ways of prying open shells to youngsters, who pass the tradition on in turn: birds with inventiveness and culture, if you are willing to allow them such. And even, or especially, paddlers upset them. "Don't cause an animal to alter its behavior," goes the slogan for the person who wants only to watch and not trespass upon creatures besides man, but some of them set tests for us which every time we almost surely fail. There are some skills to paddling beyond the strokes and rolls that seem to take a life to learn. This book, I hope, will not make the oystercatchers' lives any harder than they are, or the lives of all the other shy companions on the bay.

Later, like a flash of revelation, it became clear to me: There are only three American oystercatchers in the bay. Those birds seen on Spar Island in Mount Hope Bay, the ones that others have seen flying south along the midline of the Sakonnet River north of Gould Island, those seen on tiny Greene's Island by Occupassatuxet Cove, those beside Hope Island, and now the ones by Coggeshall's Point are all the same, or if not the very same then the sum population of oyster-catchers in the bay at that time. Their flight is fast, they think nothing of flying half the length of the bay, they choose to alight on deserted sandbars, an uncommon habitat, they flee from any hint of people? If there were any more in the bay, a person cruising the bay's shorelines by kayak would see or hear them fleeing from some other place. All right then; maybe there are six, or even nine, two or three groups of three. Still, not many individuals of a species that is said to be established here. Do we appreciate how thinly spread our wildlife is, what damage the loss of one piece of habitat can do, the impact of one death upon a race?

A wooden hulk sits offshore in the angle north of Coggeshall's Point. Whatever it used to be, it seems not to have spread timbers, spikes, or other traps into the water nearby, so a paddler can slide around to either side. A little farther north, well in toward shore, whaleback boulders with barnacle armor could shred a hull's bright finish; there are few enough that once seen they can be dodged.

Watertrail 5A, Link 1: Cory's Lane to Willow Lane

Presuming that you have found a mild day to paddle from the end of Cory's Lane, head north not far outside the rocks that guard this shore. The tidal current strengthens rapidly with distance from the shore and there are numerous onshore details to be seen. A small stone building, perched between the wooded banking and the rocks, attracts the eye: Is it a studio or a boathouse?

Some rocks loose on the shore or in the outcrops beneath the browline of the vegetated banking are deeply black. There's metaanthracite coal along here; Portsmouth was once one source of this "Rhode Island coal," occasionally maligned for its reluctance to ignite.

Look ahead along the shore for the tall, skeletal framework of a building rising from a field at the base of the broad swath of land that projects west into the bay. In 1966, as excavation for a factory at that site was beginning, an earthmover dropped some distance into the ground. It had fallen through the roof of a gallery of the old abandoned Aquedneck [sic] Coal Mine, which was incorporated in 1809 and operated until 1913. When you reach the next landing and launching spot, the beach at the end of Willow Lane, pick up a shell and see which of the many black stones are soft enough to leave a mark on it; you'll have a piece of Rhode Island coal (which will burn, just) or graphite (which will not).

Before reaching that point of land, though, you'll paddle past (or underneath; it seems quite safe) a long pier stretching from the shore in front of two tremendous wood chalets, and before and beyond them there are resting spots, sand or gravel beaches, the first one beneath tree cover and the more northern one in front of fields.

Move out along the westward curving shore at the north end of this

Fig. 85 *Willow Lane launching beach as seen from the water*

long embayment and notice the stonework promontory that extends from the corner where the coast comes north again. There's a tongue of low rocks that runs south some 10 or 15 yards from the tip of this construction, so leave at least several boat lengths between yourself and this jetty. Low tide is a good time to admire the design and workmanship of this stone pier, which seems to be unique in the bay system, although small versions exist in the Sakonnet north of Fogland *(fig. 85)*.

The beach north of the pier, before the shore curves out to Arnold's Point proper, dips in shallowly toward land and makes a hint of a cove. Where the pier protects the beach from waves, close to its base, the shoreline creeps out along the pier's northern side, and there paddlers will find the best landing zone, as the surface is coarse sand at all tides. More than 2 boat lengths from the pier's base the bottom exposed below high tide is stony. The farther north you go, the more you move into the frontal path of the waves. The beach is largely sandy above the high-tide wrack.

Watertrail 5A, Launching Site 2: Willow Lane Beach

Willow Lane leads down to Arnold's Point, which is a fascinating piece of shoreline, with remains of a stone wharf unique in the bay, and low cliffs, paths, and wonderful views. The sheltered beach north of the wharves serves paddlers well as a launching site in a part of the bay that otherwise is not easy to enter.

Willow Lane Beach: Driving

From Bristol, cross the Mount Hope Bridge, go straight (more accurately, slightly to the right) through the intersection, continue for 1.2 miles to an intersection with a traffic light and get in the right-hand lane. Turn right with Rhode Island RI 114. Willow Lane is the first street to the right. Follow it to its end at the water's edge, and park along the border of the field or in a parking space around the opening in the fence to the right.

From the south, come north along RI 114 and pass Cory's Lane with its signs for the topiary gardens, school, and abbeys. Willow Lane is about 1.5 miles farther along on the left.

Willow Lane Beach: Launching

There are four or more paths to the beach from the margins of the dirt road and the field, but the easiest seems to be the one that is not quite half the field's width from the field's northwest corner, where the road is nearest the water and bends to the right past a section of chain-link fence. Beware the ditch (filled with a line of hay bales) that goes along the field's western, beachside border.

About halfway from where this short path opens onto the beach and the base of the rock wharves to the left (south), paddlers will find a short stretch of sandy beach well suited to launching and landing

Fig. 86 *Section of the Willow Lane beach best suited to launching and landing*

kayaks tucked into the lee of the wharf out of wind and waves coming up the throat of the East Passage *(fig. 86)*.

Once beyond the lee of the wharves, a paddler should take honest stock of the conditions. The wave patterns here can sometimes seem to have ill intentions, and paddling in them may not be relaxing at all. On other days, it is idyllic. As this site is along Watertrail 5A, not really at an end, paddlers can head either north or south along the coast. Going north, stay close to shore; consult the charts to appreciate how close the channel comes to Arnold's Point. When heading south, stay east of a line from Arnold's Point to Coggeshall's Point, that is, maintain a heading of less than 214 degrees magnetic.

Watertrail 5A, Loop 2: Willow Lane Beach around Arnold's Point to Portsmouth Terminal, and Return

Even on a day when the south wind holds flags almost straight out, a quick trip around Arnold's Point will put a kayaker in the lee of land and alongside interesting shorefront features: outcrops of the local coal-bearing rocks, small houses with their faces pressed up against the bay, the remains of an old stone bridge fronted by a picnic-perfect beach, and a wharf with such varied visitors as a barge claiming to be laden with fireworks and a gloss-white ground-effect craft said to speed across the water at 130 mph, 6 feet above the waves. A glorious view of the Mount Hope Bridge adds to the attractions of this brief curlicue at the north end of the West Aquidneck watertrail *(fig. 87)*.

Fig. 87 *Rounding the northwest corner of Arnold's Point*

Watertrail 5B: Bristol Harbor

*K*AYAKERS SEEKING relaxation love harbors, and if one had to rank the bay's harbors on safety, variety, and scenery, the top spot just might go to Bristol Harbor, which has the diversity of Wickford without the traffic, the historic and aesthetic sailboats of Newport without the waves, the placidity of Dutch Island Harbor but with a lively waterfront, and so on. Paddlers who want to explore beyond the mooring grounds have Usher's Cove, Poppasquash Point, and Hog Island all within a 2-NM radius of the launching site.

Watertrail 5B, Launching Site 1: Bristol Northern Town Boat Ramp

There are other public access points around Bristol Harbor, but the beach and parking area at the northeast corner of the harbor by the town boat ramp are so perfectly constructed and located for paddlers that there seems to be no reason, at least at present, to mention others.

Bristol Northern Town Boat Ramp: Driving

Proceed on RI 114 to the north end of downtown Bristol. Go south of a tidal brook that passes under RI 114. Take Thames Street, which forks off to the harbor side of the business district. Make an immediate right to enter the ramp and launching beach area; the best parking is ahead at the top of the low rise, facing the trees.

Bristol Northern Town Boat Ramp: Launching

There are no special considerations in this area other than to watch for powerboat traffic approaching from around the end of the wharf to the

Fig. 88 *Bristol Town Boat Ramp from the water, with kayaker*

left of the beach, where the view is blocked. Consequently, when heading away from the beach, keep your boat some distance from the wharf. Other than that, this site opens onto the inner end of a sheltered harbor *(fig. 88)*.

Watertrail 5B, Loop 1: Bristol Northern Town Boat Ramp to Poppasquash Point, and Return

Paddling close to the shore from the launching site to Poppasquash Point, a 2.7-NM one-way trip, will carry you past lovely homes, sweet antique sailboats, and inviting small beaches in nooks between stands of spartina. Additionally, encounters with fellow paddlers, boaters, swimmers, and wildlife make this route about as pleasant a jaunt around a harbor's edge as could be imagined. Most days a paddler makes this trip more to enjoy the sights along the way than actually to arrive at Poppasquash Point, but if that is in fact your destination, then you may quite safely cross Bristol Harbor anywhere before it widens, which is much the same as crossing wherever boats are thickly moored, at least in warmer months. For scenery and variety, however, head further north into the harbor from the ramp, and swing in close to the stone walls, grasses, rocks, and bushes; you'll see dragonflies and swallows chasing down small insects on the wing. Perhaps an American egret will sway to and fro on the leader of a sapling barely large enough to bear its weight *(fig. 89)*.

Fig. 89 *North end of Bristol Harbor*

Having curved around the head of the harbor and begun south along Poppasquash Neck, one encounters piers extending from the shore and dense boat moorings once again. Currently, there's a kayak rental business along here, too, about where the road bends away from the water.

The sailboats moored along this route alone are worth the trip. Every time you go through this press of boats, another sailboat delights the eyes: it could be a stark red flat-out racer or one designed by Nathaniel Greene Herreshoff with such grace and perfection of line as to seem somehow aerodynamic, if that were possible.

Farther south, the moorings end and just woods and residences glide by on shore. Round the end of Usher's Neck, the thumb of Poppasquash Neck's mitten, and enter Usher's Cove, then curve left toward the south again. Somewhere along this shore, you may wish to stop to rest or read or watch a hermit crab; there are a handful of miniature

Fig. 90 *Heading north up the east side of Poppasquash Neck and boats in Bristol Harbor*

Fig. 91 *Just off the end of Poppasquash Point*

beaches in the gaps between the spartina stands and in the shade of trees. First come, first served *(fig. 90)*.

You'll know Poppasquash Point by the most unusual sight of one boulder sitting partway on and partway off another. What an odd place to find a glacial erratic perched rock. Was somebody with a dredging barge feeling whimsical, or was this caused by heaving ice floes driven by huge winter waves? *(fig. 91)*

Beyond this pair of rocks, 100 yards or so, the water changes. (This is as far as this book's suggested tour takes you.)

Hog Island lies so near off to the left it seems a shame to miss it, but on this crossing strange waves and fast boats are the rule. Also, Hog Island actually is over half a nautical mile away. It is much better to approach Hog Island from the eastern side, from the other side of the harbor *(fig. 92)*.

While returning to the starting point, feel free to cut across the mouth of Usher's Cove but delay cutting across the harbor until well

Fig. 92 *Boat traffic in the channel between Poppasquash Neck and Hog Island*

among the moored boats. You must still keep a sharp watch for sailboats underway and busy launches that shuttle between the boats and
shore. The safer way to go is to delay crossing the harbor until opposite
the launching ramp.

Watertrail 5B, Loop 2: Bristol Northern Town Boat Ramp to Bristol Point, perhaps Hog Island, and Return

Heading left (south) once clear of the launching beach takes a paddler
past the waterfront of Bristol along a narrow water corridor between
pier ends and wharves on one hand and the boat channel just yards
away on the other; groups stay tight and leaders and tailboats stay alert.
Watch for surprise arrivals and departures to and from the waterfront:
the Prudence Island ferry service keeps an active schedule. Do not
count on a ferry large enough to carry a school bus being able to slow
down or swerve if a paddler gets in its way!

Fig. 93 *Kayakers and moored boats along the Bristol waterfront*

Beyond the close-set piers, conditions settle down *(fig. 93)*, and
paddlers can look forward to 1.5 NM or more of wonderful sights and
sounds: green sloping lawns, social life on shore, crews in sailboats getting underway, small antique jewels of historic boat design, and approaching in the south the towers, curves, and taut lines of the Mount
Hope Bridge.

On the way out or back, dip in behind grassy Walker's Island,
minding rocks and pilings, for a respite from the wind and waves, if
needed *(fig. 94)*.

Fig. 94 *Little Walker's Island, 1.2 NM south of launching site 1 in Bristol Harbor*

When the shore begins to curve away to the left (southeast), come to a stop or coast, look carefully ahead, and consider. In this book's opinion, the waters that a paddler sees now begin to be truly dangerous, and a prudent paddler should stay behind the breakwater that extends from shore at this southwest corner of Bristol Point, before the bridge *(fig. 95)*.

The safest way for a paddler to get to and from Hog Island may be to go about 0.3 NM north along the shoreline from the northern tip of Walker's Island (or 0.3 NM south of the town pier or 0.15 NM south of the Coast Guard Station) and look due magnetic east for the red-green buoy that marks where the harbor channel divides to pass east and west of Hog Island. Come and go to the island along the line that connects your position to the buoy. Recall that Hog Island may be sheltering your party from conditions to the south and that the south side of the island may be quite different from the north. Those interested in birds might be rewarded if they bring along waterproof binoculars and approach the islets and sand spits north of the main part of Hog Island quietly; would someone please identify those sparrows hiding in the beach grass?

Fig. 95 *Bristol Point at the north end of Mount Hope Bridge*

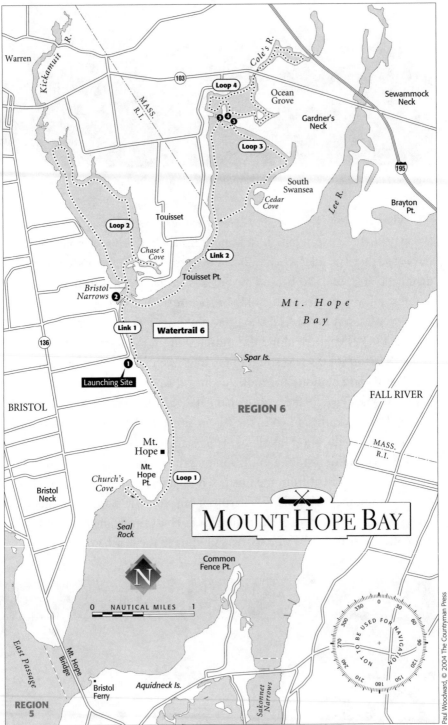

Warren

Kickamuit R.

MASS. R.I.

103

Loop 4

Cole's R.

Ocean Grove

Sewammock Neck

3 4 5

Gardner's Neck

Loop 3

South Swansea

Cedar Cove

Lee R.

195

Brayton Pt.

Loop 2

Touisset

Chase's Cove

Link 2

Touisset Pt.

Mt. Hope Bay

Bristol Narrows

2

Link 1

136

Watertrail 6

Spar Is.

1

Launching Site

BRISTOL

REGION 6

FALL RIVER

MASS. R.I.

Mt. Hope

Mt. Hope Pt.

Loop 1

Bristol Neck

Church's Cove

Seal Rock

Common Fence Pt.

MOUNT HOPE BAY

N

0   NAUTICAL MILES   1

NOT TO BE USED FOR NAVIGATION

0 30 60 90 120 150 180 210 240 270 300 330

East Passage

Mt. Hope Bridge

Bristol Ferry

Aquidneck Is.

Sakonnet Narrows

REGION 5

Paul Woodward, © 2004 The Countryman Press

Watertrail 6: Mount Hope Bay and Tributaries, from Church's Cove to Cole's River

*T*HIS WATERTRAIL along the west and northwest margins of Mount Hope Bay and two tributary rivers may be the richest in wildlife and natural attractions. Also, as overdeveloped and urbanized as much of Bristol Neck on the west side of Mount Hope Bay and Fall River on the east are, bits of the countryside lie in between. This at least awakens the hope that fragments of the land the way the Narragansetts saw it in the days of Roger Williams, and before, still remain.

Watertrail 6, Launching Site 1: Mount Hope Fishing Area

The Mount Hope Fishing Area provides parking, a ramp, and at least at low tide a sand flat along the western shore of Mount Hope Bay. The immediate waters are not as tricky or congested as at the Bristol Narrows 0.5 NM north, so paddlers accustomed to launching from the narrows may want to try this site, and paddlers who have tried neither can introduce themselves to a lightly visited part of the bay system.

Mount Hope Fishing Area: Driving

Follow Metacom Avenue (RI 136) to the Rhode Island Veterans' Home on the east side of the road; look for two artillery pieces painted white in a grassy field and a Bristol fire station named "Hydraulion" set back from Metacom Avenue. At the T-intersection just north of these landmarks, Annawamscutt Drive goes east directly to Mount Hope Bay. Follow Annawamscutt Drive almost to the end; look for a sign to MOUNT HOPE FISHING AREA on the right (just before Camp Crosby). Turn right (south) onto the unpaved access road to the fishing area and drive to the end, where there's a parking lot with room for up to 20 cars, launching beaches, and a ramp.

Mount Hope Fishing Area: Launching

If no one is the area when you arrive, and if you quietly approach the shrubs separating the parking lot from the beach and then the beach and grasses, you may see warblers, sparrows, sandpipers, horseshoe crabs, and a small flock of brants (a small goose about the size of a mallard). The right (south) side of the ramp usually makes the easiest

Fig. 96 *Mount Hope Fishing Area, seen from the water*

launching; if the tide is quite low, the flat that is exposed a little farther from shore at that side usually is firm and clean as is the submerged bottom beside it *(fig. 96).*

Due east magnetic from this launching site lies what is probably the longest east-west traverse of Mount Hope Bay—over 3.1 NM to the opposite shore. Experienced paddlers that make the crossing here must first cross the boat channel that lies just off the western shore of Mount

Hope Bay; then the open water; and third, a shipping channel into Fall River near the other side that still sees some merchant traffic.

Heading north or south alongshore, particularly in the morning before the wind has begun to howl, however, is delightful. Paddlers seeking relaxation will not go south all the way to Bristol Point to the south; the beach inside Church's Cove around Mount Hope Point is probably the choicest destination in this direction.

To the north one has the Bristol Narrows launching site, the Kicka-muit River, and Cole's River, too, all lovely to explore. The principal difficulty in proceeding north involves avoiding boat traffic in the channel south of the narrows, which lies astonishingly close to the shore, but this can be dealt with by paddling right in among the moored boats and spartina.

Watertrail 6, Loop 1: Mount Hope Fishing Area to Church's Cove, and Return

If there's any place around the bay that can take us back beyond even our colonial history, it is Mount Hope, a governmental seat of the Nar-ragansetts, which rises 200 feet above the shore. While there are a few higher hills in and around the bay (Pocasset Hill in Tiverton, Drum Rock Hill in Warwick, the central spine of Aquidneck Island), none has Mount Hope's privileged central location in the bay, from which a

Fig. 97 *East side of Bristol Neck south of Mount Hope Fishing Area launch site; here, Brown University students assess the bay's health*

sharp eye could detect events on Conanicut, other center of Narragansett government, 15 NM away. In turn, Mount Hope can be clearly seen on the skyline from the mouth of the Sakonnet River, an almost equal distance *(fig. 97)*.

So, along this loop you'll glide beside the highest, steepest shore that you'll can encounter on these watertrails, matched in pitch only by the slopes north of McCorrie's Point along Watertrail 7A on the Sakonnet River.

The hillside, however, does not continue underwater. The tidal zone around Mount Hope is friendly. Along the shore are narrow strips of salt marsh and stony beaches where you can pause and perhaps pull out your boats.

Watertrail 6, Link 1:
Mount Hope Fishing Area to Bristol Narrows

The hop between these two launching sites is short, barely 0.6 NM, but deserves some care and caution between about the halfway mark and the narrows due to the unusual placement of the boat channel, which lies practically in the shadow of the shore. Boats heading for the narrows from the southern parts of the bay converge toward the western shoreline while maintaining wake-generating speed, sometimes giving a kayaker no warning when closing from behind; they may keep enough separation to avoid collisions but little more than that. A kayaker who is not in among the boat moorings along this stretch should be on high alert *(fig. 98)*.

The line of red nun buoys marking the offshore side of this channel

Fig. 98 *Bristol Narrows from the offshore side of the channel*

Fig. 99 View from Bristol Narrows south along east side of Bristol Neck
toward the Mount Hope Fishing Area launch site

is a scant 150 to 200 feet from shore, by the chart; the channel lies shoreward of them and moorings are squeezed in between the channel and
the shore. Despite having all of Mount Hope Bay spread out to the east,
one might as well be tiptoeing between the piers in a marina *(fig. 99)*.

At the narrows, it is possible to land on the open, eastern shore of
the sandbar exposed when the tide is low. The inner side of the bar and
the steeper part used by boat trailers are accessible by continuing to the
narrow ribbon of deeper water that wraps around the sandbar's north
end. Even at midtide there may not be enough water over the bar to
float a kayak, although a canoe might just glide across. The passage
around the end of the bar, however, is shared with powerboats and Jet
Skis. Keep your guard up until onshore.

Watertrail 6, Launching Site 2: Bristol Narrows

The Bristol Narrows seems to be the most popular launching spot for
paddlers in the western half of Mount Hope Bay. There are parking
spots for a dozen cars and sandy beaches for launching and landing.
Paddlers have to pay attention to the peculiar, compressed mix of boat
traffic, currents, and shoals if they're to avoid surprises, though.

Bristol Narrows: Driving

Drive north or south into Bristol on RI 136 (Metacom Avenue). Turn east
at the intersection marked with a traffic signal where Gooding Avenue
comes from the west and Narrows Road comes from the east; you may

Fig. 100 *Looking north into Bristol Narrows*

only find the sign for Gooding. Drive almost to the end of Narrows Road, but use care especially toward the end, as the road descends sharply. Turn left onto the crooked entry road to the launching area. Park on the landward side; launch from either side of the low point of land *(fig. 100)*.

Bristol Narrows: *Launching*

The salient feature of this launching area is that as soon as you push away from the beach you and your boat are in an almost uniquely compact marine traffic environment, a miniature golf course's worth of things to dodge—currents, sandbars, shallows, channels, pilings, moorings, powerboats, and maybe even fellow paddlers—so plan the exact route that you and your party will take before you get into your boats.

 If going south along the western shore of Mount Hope Bay, hug the shore closely and use pilings, grass, and moorings for cover until almost past the housefronts overlooking the water from the street above. After that, paddlers can follow the shore more loosely.

 If heading east along the bay's northern shore toward Cole's River, then consider crossing as close to the Kickamuit River as you can, because a no-wake marker in the throat of the narrows tends to keep boat traffic slow even a short ways south of it. Then cross the channel and hug the beach on the Touisset side of the narrows until nearing the first construction, where you'll swing out to clear the first of the piers that extend from the land. After that, paddlers have plenty of room to move about all the way to Cole's River and in along its western shore.

If heading through the narrows into the Kickamuit River, begin the same way but continue along the west bank past the no-wake marker, beyond which you can choose an opportune time and place to cross to the Touisset shore, if you wish, or just follow the shore around the sharp bend to the left (west), remembering that the Kickamuit River harbors a good many boats and that they all must enter or leave the river through this one twisty passage. There are perhaps a tenth as many boats moored along the eastern shore as along the western, and there are also the attractions of secluded Chase's Cove and the "boulder garden" toward the north on the Touisset side, so the eastern shore may be more congenial for paddlers than the western.

Be prepared for the current through the narrows. Halfway between high and low tides, when tidal flow is greatest, the current tears swiftly through the narrows. Currents are usually weaker toward shore, unless an undercut banking signals otherwise.

Watertrail 6, Loop 2: Bristol Narrows into the Kickamuit River, and Return

The banks of the Kickamuit River diverge north of the narrows and converge again farther on having formed a tidal pond as much as 0.6 NM across and about 0.8 NM long. The west bank is more thickly settled than the east. On hot days, the center of the tidal pond amounts to a no-man's-land to paddlers due to the boats and, more particularly, the

Fig. 101 *Looking north along the east bank of the Kickamuit River from Chase's Cove entrance*

Jet Skis, which crisscross the pond at what appear to be 40-knot speeds. The alongshore environment, nevertheless, offers scenic, sheltered paddling, and a circuit of this tidal pond, a trip of about 2.4 NM, could be a pleasant outing at almost any time. The east bank is well sheltered from the south afternoon winds that can maul Mount Hope Bay *(fig. 101)*. The west bank runs straight for 1.1 NM of pleasant paddling, and even more if one explores the narrow, twisty part of the river to the north *(fig. 102)*. Two appendages to the pond, Chase's Cove cutting eastward into

Fig. 102 *Looking south along the more built-up west shore of the Kickamuit*

the southern Touisset shore and the narrower section of the river itself in the northwest corner of the pond, could also be explored, more readily at mid to high tide of course.

Watertrail 6, Link 2: Bristol Narrows to Cole's River Boat Ramp

Cross the channel of the Narrows and head east along the north shore of Mount Hope Bay between the mouths of the Kickamuit River and Cole's River. There are some rocks in the water early on, around the first few piers. The 0.9 NM paddle along the northeast-tending shore goes by an assortment of piers, lawns, beaches, salt marsh, a small creek, and trees artistically silhouetted against the sky *(fig. 103)*.

About 1.0 NM from the Bristol Narrows, the shore turns to exactly due true north for another 1.0 NM of paddling along a scenic shore.

Fig. 103 *Across from the south and southeast shores of Warren Neck (or Touisset Neck) toward the Cole's, Lee's, and Taunton Rivers*

Here you'll see some of the prettiest boats and houses in the bay; during one visit, they looked tidy and refreshed as they glistened from the rain. There also are nooks behind the spartina in among the rocks below the beach where a kayaker can pull in for a cozy lunch.

At the north end of this run along the shore, water hurtles through, either in or out of, the Cole's River Narrows. Cross over to be in front of the beach when you are 50 or 100 yards short of the narrows, out where the firehose current is weaker. Approach the beach somewhere between the point next to the narrows and well away from the short stretch of spartina grass that, improbably enough, gives shelter to an entire community of shorebirds, or go beyond to the right (east) to the beginning of the Swansea Town Beach.

Watertrail 6, Launching Site 3: Swansea Town Beach and Cole's River Boat Ramp

Use either the Swansea Town Beach's farthest (westernmost) parking lot and path to the shore or the Swansea Town Boat Ramp's small beaches to launch kayaks and canoes into Cole's River where it widens before entering Mount Hope Bay. To launch toward the upstream part of the river, use the actual boat ramp or the low ground beside it.

Swansea Town Beach and Cole's River Boat Ramp: Driving

Proceed east or west on RI 103 through Swansea, Massachusetts. If coming from the intersection of I-195 and RI 103 at Exit 4, drive west to cross Lee's River then Gardner's Neck Road. If coming from Warren or Luther's Corners, then east to cross Cole's River.

Between Gardner's Neck Road and Cole's River, Macomber Ave, goes south from RI 103; at its intersection is the sign for SWANSEA TOWN BEACH. Follow the signs for the beach: They lead right onto Elmwood Avenue, which curves left, right again onto another street, which makes another left curve, then right onto Ocean Grove Avenue.

It is possible and also nondisruptive to the juvenal shorebirds to launch from the beach. Turn in the entrance, pay, and go all the way to the last parking lot; use one of the last paths to the beach to get your boat and gear to the water. Beach parking costs $5.

To go to the boat ramp, go past the entrance to the beach on your left, through a dogleg where the road jogs south, and out the sand spit to the boat ramp parking lot.

Getting out of Ocean Park can be tricky, as some of the streets that brought you from Macomber to the beach are one-way, and the way back to RI 103 is not marked; turn left after the intersection that brought you to Ocean Grove Avenue and bear left at a fork that soon follows and you should be able to escape from Ocean Park eventually.

Seasonal passes to use the boat ramp lot, whether for parking or launching with or without using the ramp, are currently $15 for residents of Swansea or $35 for nonresidents and are obtainable at the town hall. Day passes cost $5 on weekdays, $8 on weekends and holidays. Take an envelope from the green box at the entrance to the parking lot, seal a filled-out form and a check in the envelope, drop through the slot in the locked part of the box, and hang the tag that you found in the envelope from your inside rearview mirror. It is not an honor system: Police patrol frequently and look for the tags, write down plate numbers, and so on. Vehicles without trailers should be parked at the landward end of the lot, away from the ramp end.

From the boat ramp lot, canoes and kayaks can be launched either from the beach to the left beyond the ramp end of the lot or from the beach about halfway along the parking lot: Try to stay away from the sea grass. The ramp is also fine for launching and landing; it appears to be inclined less steeply than most big concrete ramps and has a floating walkway along each side.

Swansea Town Beach and Cole's River Boat Ramp: Launching

Looking south toward Mount Hope Bay, from the Swansea Town Beach or the town's boat-launching area, two arms, Gardner's Neck on the left (east) and Warren or Touisset Neck on the right (west), stretch wide apart and then approach each other to form the mouth of Cole's River, almost exactly 0.5 NM wide *(fig. 104)*.

Making a circuit of the entire shoreline in one loop is as pleasant and varied a short (2.6 NM) trip as the bay offers but requires crossing a half mile of open water and a lightly used boat channel. Even in good weather, conditions at the mouth of the river can be demanding, in keeping with the personality of Mount Hope Bay; try not to make the crossing if there's any chance that anyone in your party would be over-matched by the wind and water. Better to simply turn around and return the way you came. Since kayakers, for example, rarely turn right around while seated in their boat, they at least are likely to see something they missed when traveling in the opposite direction.

Fig. 104 *Path to Swansea Town Beach from parking lot: no currents here*

Paddling out along the side of Warren Neck takes you straight to the mouth in about 0.7 NM along a wooded shore with lovely houses and a few attractive small boats, but you'll be exposed to any south wind.

The other route, alongside Gardner's Neck, goes almost twice the distance (about 1.4 NM) to reach the river's mouth, which is well marked by a point of land on this side. The conditions along this route are likely to be stiffest right at the outset and milder thereafter, because after Swansea Town Beach the rest of the shoreline is sheltered from the south by the west-pointing boot toe of Gardner's Neck.

A word about wildlife: Nearly three dozen young semipalmated plovers were learning to make a living from the spartina clumps and small sand flats south of the launching site parking lot during mid-August. Almost as many juvenal lesser yellowlegs were similarly occupied, but they operated in groups of three or four, not all together as the little plovers commonly did, and jumped on each other and squabbled over tidbits like squirrels beneath a birdfeeder *(fig. 105)*.

Offshore, 14-inch-long bluefish thrashed and churned the water into spray and upwellings; while the onslaught lasted, up to four fish were in the air at once. Along the opposite side of the river was a fortune in shorebirds, even an elegant black-bellied plover in full formal

Fig. 105　*Semipalmated plovers call the spartina and sandflats home*

dress, plus a harrier kiting in tight twists and turns above the sandbar and saw grass not 10 feet from the boat.

The launching site at Cole's River generously gives paddlers a "twofer," because not only can one go around the small bay to the south but one also has immediately to the north an intricately cut playground of inlets and islands as well as the mainstream of Coles's River itself, which seems benign, clean, and most attractive.

Watertrail 6, Loop 3: Swansea Town Beach or Cole's River Boat Ramp to Mouth of Cole's River, and Return by Other Side

Launch toward the south, the bay side and, on a flood tide, make some distance from the beach before cutting west toward the high, wooded shore to avoid the current accelerating toward the gap; on an ebb tide, the current can give a boat a boost for some distance before it dissipates.

Watch for fish, birds, and aesthetically pleasing boats and houses (*fig. 106*). Toward the mouth of the river the shore begins to bend to the

Fig. 106 *West bank of Cole's River between Swansea Town Boat Ramp and the river's mouth*

Fig. 107 *West side of the mouth of Cole's River with Mount Hope*

west and a small false point appears with silhouetted trees, boulders off-shore, and beds of spartina *(fig. 107)*. Gauge here whether to cross the river's mouth to the point of land opposite. The distance across is about 0.42 NM on a course of 85 to 90 degrees magnetic. Be visible. Perhaps switch on a strobe light attached to your boat's deck while crossing. Be ready to be audible: Have your whistle accessible on its lanyard or between your teeth. Be alert: Keep checking to both sides.

Having crossed, swing left back into Cole's River alongside the sandy shore topped with beach grass past the entrance to Cedar Cove, in among the boat moorings, then out the other side and over toward the shore on the right, the west side of Gardner's Neck.

Come north along the fronts of cottages protected by walls against the waves and then curve back toward the starting spot by passing in front of the Swansea town beach, which, when it is empty of people, may attract hundreds of gulls and, oddly enough, dozens of ruddy turnstones (a bird in the plover family).

If landing at the boat ramp area, go well beyond the spartina at the other end of the beach before putting in to shore; consider landing on the sand just before the end of the point of land beyond the parking lot. Coasting past the spartina making no sound may earn a look at a remarkable local concentration of shorebirds.

Watertrail 6, Loop 4: Swansea Town Beach or Cole's River Boat Ramp to Upstream Waters, and Return

Rather than landing after completing the preceding loop, paddlers may wish to line up with the gap between the two points beyond the boat ramp parking lot and pass through into the upstream river where there's a baroque shoreline, plus cozy views in every direction and an island to circle. The river is said to be navigable beyond the first highway bridge as far as the second, which carries I-195 across the river and at high tide particularly this may well be so *(fig. 108)*.

Fig. 108 *Islet in Cole's River upstream of the narrows, as seen from the boat ramp lot*

Scheduling a paddle to the upstream Cole's River centered around high tide would have the advantage of having the current with one both ways through the gap at the launching area, as well as making the greatest area accessible to the boats. Paddlers who do not want to have to cope with the current through the gap at all can use the actual boat ramp or the sandy or grassy areas to either side of it for launching and landing *(fig. 109)*.

Fig. 109 *Narrows at Cole's River*

Watertrail 7A: Aquidneck Island Side of the Sakonnet River

A PADDLER looking at a chart of Narragansett Bay for a large area of calm and untried water, although perhaps with not much hope of succeeding, might be amazed to find the sheltered expanse 1.75 square NM large (2.5 NM by 0.7 NM) in the northwest corner of the Sakonnet River's "vik." Access from the west has only been found at Sandy Point, but remarkably along the northern edge there are five points of entry open to the public, and paddlers will find that the one closest to the center of these headwaters could hardly be better for launching and landing their crafts.

Watertrail 7A, Launching Site 1: Sandy Point on Aquidneck Island

Public access to the shore along the east side of Aquidneck is sparse at best. North of Third Beach on the side of Sachuest, as far south as one can be in the Sakonnet River, there's apparently only one public access stop: Sandy Lane, halfway along the Sakonnet, that is, 4.1 NM from either Flint Point on Sachuest or from Island Park's long beach in straight-line distance, perhaps as the cormorant flies.

Back in the 18th century, according to Blaskowitz's map, along the west side of the Seaconnet Passage one found Sandy Point, Fogland Ferry, and Little Sandy Point; these days, we call old Sandy Point McCorrie's Point, and Fogland Ferry has become our Sandy Point, while

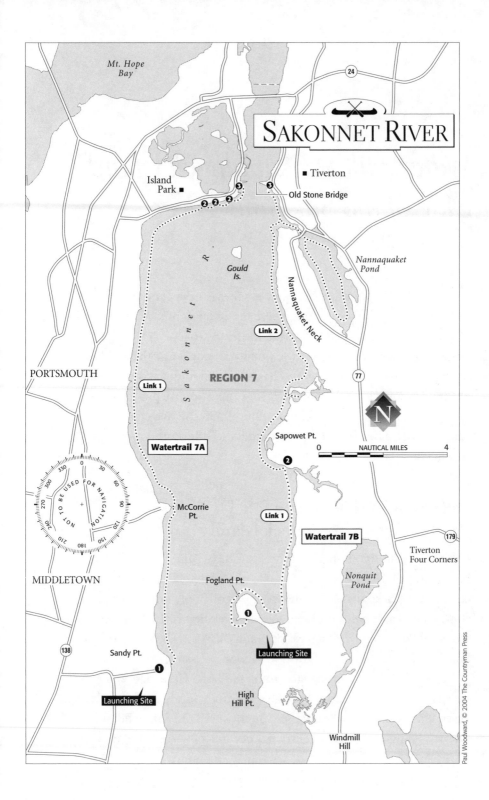

old Little Sandy Point seems to have lost its name entirely, although it is a little hard to be sure which wiggle in the map's shoreline should be associated with which present-day geographical feature. One could be tempted to think that Blaskowitz's informants were pulling his leg.

Worse yet, the 1777 map says that there were two Black Points along the Seaconnet Passage's west bank, both north and south of the two Sandy Points. Nowadays, the southern Black Point keeps the name, but the northern one on modern maps has no name at all, one solution to the problem but hardly a thorough one.

Names aside, Sandy Point on Aquidneck has ample parking and a fine beach for paddlers to use, plus in season a panoramic view in which schools of bluefish turn one patch of the river, then another, into foam.

Looking south from Sandy Point beach along the east side of Aquidneck Island, you see the lower third of the Sakonnet River. Black Point protrudes from the shore on the right, blocking from sight Third Beach, Sachuest Point, and the river's mouth almost to the westernmost of the islets off Sakonnet Point in Little Compton; where the lighthouse off Sakonnet Point peeks up along the skyline.

Sandy Point is almost across the river from Fogland Point, which is a little more than 0.5 NM farther to the north. High Hill Point, also on the other shore and south of Fogland, lies somewhat south of Sandy Point, perhaps a third of a mile. South of High Hill Point comes an apparently unnamed headland, then little Brown Point, then imposing Church's Point girt with its chain mail of flat- and round-stone steep shelving beach, which helps barricade the upstream Sakonnet against the sound.

Looking north along Aquidneck's eastern side from Sandy Point, you see McCorrie's Point jutting out from the left 1.6 NM to the north; actually, the Point itself, a low flat sandy bar, is hard to see, and it is the landward high tree-covered slope that forms the skyline. Paler, on the skyline, a fraction to the right and in line beyond the point, Mount Hope shows up 7.3 NM away. The high land to the right is Tiverton. The low land between is in part Island Park and Grinnell's Beach, which are on either side of the Sakonnet River Narrows.

Sandy Point on Aquidneck Island: Driving

Turn east off RI 138 at the intersection with traffic light and Sandy Point Road, which does not cross RI 138. Drive to the end and park in a generously sized lot. The shore end of the road goes down a steep hill and through a built-up area with children, adults, and pets on foot.

A sign at the end of the parking lot says that vehicles are not allowed to drive beyond the parking lot onto the plateau above the beach, but this restriction is not honored by everyone. Use discretion in bringing your boat to the water, but do park in the lot.

Aquidneck's Sandy Point provides the only public access to the Sakonnet River between the north and south ends of its western shore.

Sandy Point on Aquidneck Island: Launching

Sandy Point is the middle of three points along the Sakonnet River's west shore. Black Point lies to its south and prevents much of the wave energy that enters the river from passing north of it. After the north side of Sandy Point comes a modest embayment, followed by McCorrie's Point, which shelters the river shore to the north to create a stretch of mild alongshore paddling, which should, with any luck, be trouble-free.

Distance is perhaps the chief obstacle along this watertrail; with no public access between Sandy Point and Island Park, about 4.8 NM separates Sandy Point and the access paths in Island Park if a paddler keeps close to shore, which is the distance (along Watertrail 1A) from South Ferry to the entrance to Wickford Harbor or (along Watertrail 3A) from Longmeadow to Pawtuxet Harbor.

On the other hand, looping north out of Sandy Point, launching and beaching from the same place, or looping southwest out of Island Park brings a paddler into some of the finest gentle saltwater paddling in the entire bay system.

Watertrail 7A, Link 1: Sandy Point to McCorrie's Point

The 1.4 NM long run from Sandy Point up to McCorrie's Point is easy and pleasant. At Sandy Point the Sakonnet River channel runs just off-

Fig. 110 *Aquidneck's Sandy Point seen from the north, a short distance along Watertrail 7A*

shore, but it angles across the river as you go north; by about 0.5 NM north of McCorrie's Point it has crossed entirely to the other side and is shaving past Sapowet Point *(fig. 110)*.

The land on this west side of the river rises steeply to 140 feet above the river, and a paddler can be in shadow relatively early in the afternoon, but the water and the opposite shore can also glow with the reflected light of a prolonged sunset. Paddlers may be interested in observing whether my experience repeats itself: The waves that reach into the hollow between Sandy Point and McCorrie's Point were highest every twelfth to fifteenth wave, dying down to a nearly calm surface midway between the high amplitude groups. A paddler might want to keep count and glance behind to check the height of the next group about to overtake the boat. Paddlers of flattish-bottomed boats could probably catch a surfing ride on some of these peaks.

Bluefish swarm up through schools of minnows along the river, and often a paddler will find the water's surface being ripped and slashed only a few yards away, soon to be visited by gulls come for the leavings. Up on a high dock along this shore a man was cleaning a sizeable fish that had a tail like the sliver before a new moon; when asked what kind of fish it was, he replied happily that he had a bluefin tuna caught some forty miles offshore, a stranger reeled in from a different world.

Check for half a dozen sea ducks around McCorrie's Point as you approach; the neighborhood always seems to feature a few scoters, white-winged ones on occasion.

Watertrail 7A, Resting and Emergency Recovery Site 1: McCorrie's Point

McCorrie's Point marks the southern extent along the western shore of the relatively placid waters in the northwest angle of the Sakonnet and so would be an ideal launching site along Watertrail 7A. Its access road and parking spaces do not seem to be open to the public, though, and this guide can only recommend McCorrie's Point as a resting spot and an emergency boat-recovery spot for paddlers. For these purposes, it is ideal.

McCorrie's Point: Driving

At the traffic light on RI 138, turn east onto McCorry's Lane (note spelling differs from McCorrie's Point). Drive to end; caution: steep hill and pedestrians. No nonresident parking is allowed, but perhaps the location could be kept in mind for use in an emergency. There's excellent access to the beach by foot.

McCorrie's Point: Launching

Since there's no parking for nonresidents, this section might be better titled "Lunching at McCorrie's Point," for this sandy point of land is conveniently located to be an interim destination for paddlers who may have set out from Sandy Point and want to explore the big northwest

Fig. 111 *From McCorrie's Point north along east side of Aquidneck Island to the 0.8-NM-long, southward-facing beach fronting Island Park*

angle of the Sakonnet. The beach here would probably be easier on boat bottoms than the rest of the shore to the north, which tends to be rocky, and the view of the river and of the western shore in particular is better, with the slight elevation of the beach and the effect that sitting on a point gives of being in a stable boat offshore.

I know of no special considerations for the water around the point: no unusual currents, depths, traffic, or other hazards *(fig. 111)*.

Watertrail 7A, Link 2: McCorrie's Point to Island Park

From McCorrie's Point to Public Access Path #1, the westernmost, is 3.5 NM measured close in to the shore. Directly point-to-point the separation is 2.8 NM along a course of 23 degrees magnetic. The direct route does not cross water with unusual currents or depths; there's a sunken wreck 0.25 NM out from McCorrie's Point shown on the chart, but that seems unlikely to concern a paddler. Between the direct course and the land to the west, providing conditions in the river are calm, a

Fig. 112 *Series of old rock constructions along the west bank of the Sakonnet River north of McCorrie's Point*

Fig. 113 *Island Park stretches two-thirds of the way across the north end of the Sakonnet River*

paddler's playground spreads out, about the size of Greenwich Bay but with better water quality and far fewer boats. The sole disadvantage is that the distance between access points is so long, 4.9 NM of shoreline, roughly, from public access at Sandy Point to the next one all the way up in Island Park. This makes one of the longest stretches of inaccessible shoreline bordering paddlecraft-friendly water in the Narragansett Bay system; indeed, it may be the longest. This corner of the bay could be a favored paddling locale were McCorrie's Point or another place within a mile and a half to its north to be opened to the public for the purpose of launching and landing canoes and kayaks *(figs. 112, 113)*.

Island Park back in the early decades of the last century was actually a park of the amusement kind, with Ferris wheel and rides and honky-tonk cafés, as much fun in one place for the navy's cruiser and destroyer crews in Newport as Aquidneck could provide, until the 1938 hurricane pushed a flood before it up the Sakonnet that swept across narrow Island Park and scattered its attractions up Mount Hope Bay as far as Fall River. Island Park sighed and settled into a quieter sort of life, but even so could not evade its own geography: Hurricane Carol in

1954 bowled up the long straight alley of the Sakonnet and knocked down many of the pins that '38 had left standing. The house of a man who was telling me this stands front and center in Island Park's waterfront with space around it where other houses used to be, but tough and hopeful to outlast the worst, as it's built of brick with half-inch steel behind the brick and armored roll-down shutters: Try to find a summer cottage built like that beside your local millpond! And even with no hurricanes in sight, the Sakonnet fills its grisly demands. We lost six this year at the narrows, said the man; fishermen, tried to anchor where they shouldn't, weren't wearing lifejackets. I just came across there from Grinnell's Beach, I said, and by the middle was wishing I had more experience; in one place the waves looked like they were playing "Ring Around the Rosy," in another there were no waves at all, just this smooth boil, up in the center, down at the edges. Forget steering—just get across. Well, Island Park is coming back, he said; there's a renaissance. No, nobody would mind if people used the public access paths. Be nice to fill that great hole in the ramp, we agreed.

Watertrail 7A, Launching Sites 2: Shoreline Public Access Paths in Island Park

In some other places around the bay, the Shoreline Public Access program has been implemented in a way that is of little use to paddlers. In Island Park, however, Shoreline Public Access comes into its own: Imagine being allowed to take your boat between two houses to an old but serviceable ramp into clean bay water and to have parking nearby, too *(fig. 114).*

Shoreline Public Access Paths in Island Park: Driving

The west end of Park Avenue goes east from RI 138; watch for the sign to Island Park. Drive east on Park Avenue along the long beach at the north end of the river and beside a low wall and sidewalk. As soon as small stores and houses appear between Park Avenue and the water, look for Gould Avenue, a side street to the south that leads to Seaconnet Boulevard, which parallels the waterfront. Four Shoreline Public Access markers are spaced along Seaconnet Boulevard.

Path #1: This westernmost Shoreline Public Access path is at the west end of Seaconnet Boulevard, which parallels Park Avenue on the south side along the eastern third of the south-facing shore of Island Park. The access path does not go across the lawn beside the support, which ends in a seawall, but is several yards to the right, across the edge of a parking lot. It goes through grass and flowers and connects to a paved parking area and the beach. This is probably the most convenient of the four, because there seems to be more parking area than the lot's users occupy during an average day. Also, the path is not steep and provides good footing for carrying a boat *(figs. 114, 115)*.

Path #2: The next path leads beside a house down to a ramp in good repair but slick below the midtide level. Parking spots may be found along the street, but a better solution would be to use the lot at the end of the street. This path is almost directly in line with the end of Gould Avenue.

Path #3: The third path descends from the middle front of a mixed bare ground and grass parking area but leads down to a rather steep concrete ramp with a large uneven hole that might endanger a person carrying a boat. The parking lot

Fig. 114 *Island Park Shoreline Public Access path, called here "#1," seen from offshore*

Fig. 115 *Shoreline public access path "#1"*

seems large enough and lightly enough used to tolerate several paddlers' cars without burdening the community, but asking around would always be a good idea.

Path #4: The fourth path is almost at the eastern end of Seaconnet Boulevard, across from the end of Ivy Avenue, the easternmost connecting street between Seaconnet Boulevard and Park Avenue. The path to the water is short and steep but well maintained. There's little space for parking along either shoulder; if using this path, perhaps the best nearby parking is in the lot above Path #3.

Shoreline Public Access Paths in Island Park: Launching

The west bank of the Sakonnet River at its northern end turns east through about 90 degrees and proceeds along 98 degrees magnetic for 0.8 NM, after which it jogs north a little and reaches the remains of the Old Stone Bridge on the west side of the mouth of the Sakonnet River Narrows at Almy Point. The long south-facing shore is a beach of sand and small stones.

To begin Watertrail 7A from its north end here, head west (right) along the beach. Once a paddler is in front of the sand beach, the area to the west from the beach south to McCorries's Point may be explored.

Watertrail 7A, Launching Site 3: Old Stone Bridge in Island Park

This launching place in Island Park looks the way boaters have come to expect: A paved lot with boat trailers beside broad frontage on the water. Paddlers, however, before launching here, should read the comments below about conditions at the Sakonnet River Narrows beside this beach *(fig. 116)*.

Fig. 116 *Looking east toward Grinnell's Beach across the tidal rip out of the Sakonnet Narrows*

Old Stone Bridge in Island Park: Driving

Get onto Park Avenue in Island Park. Close to the east end there's a bend, and the remains of the Old Stone Bridge are visible, with parking area and grassy lawn leading down to beach. Park where allowed (seafood restaurant and boating organization reserve some of the lot) and launch from right (southwest) end of beach.

Old Stone Bridge in Island Park: Launching

The principal concern is to stay away from the channel, which has a swift, upsetting current with standing waves and eddies. The jet of water that flows through the narrow opening at the Old Stone Bridge should provoke respect in kayakers, whether the tide is on the ebb or flood. Hug the shore to the right until you're in front of Island Park Beach.

Although paddling on a heading toward to the west of Gould Island should avoid the swifter parts of the current, the fact that the depth is 50 feet just north of Gould Island suggests strong currents close to the island. The tidal currents to the left (east) of Gould Island are shown two to three times as swift as those to the right (west) of the island on tidal current charts for the bay. The charted depths, in fact, suggest that the current's plume on the ebb and its funnel on the flood splays out from the narrows to blanket the beachfront here, and this book suggests that paddlers who do not consider themselves quite strong and well-prepared forgo launching from this site entirely and use instead, say, Shoreline Public Access path "#1" described above.

Watertrail 7B: Fogland Point to Grinnell's Beach, East Side of the Sakonnet River

W HEREAS Watertrail 7A will take you into an expanse of homogeneous water to explore, Watertrail 7B presents the opposite situation: beautiful small sheltered coves followed by narrow paddling corridors between bedrock embankments and nearly cinematic tidal currents. It is an intensely interesting stretch of water and shoreline, though, for paddler, naturalist, and historian.

Place-names along this shore are old and seem not to have jumped around as much as on the other side of the river. Fogland Point on Blaskowitz's map of 1777 is still Fogland Point. The land at its base was called Puncotest; Puncatest Neck is the name still used today. Nannaquaket Neck was Quacut; the entry into Nannaquaket Pond today is called the (very short) Quaket River. Nannaquaket Pond, though, was in 1777 Wantons Pond; perhaps there was a dunking stool onshore. The Sakonnet River Narrows were called the (also short) Pocasset River.

Of all the watertrails that this guide maps, this is probably the most varied and certainly one of the most scenic.

Watertrail 7B, Launching Site 1: Fogland Beach

Fogland Point is an extraordinary place for scenic views and wildlife, as well as for paddling, which is exhilarating probably at any time. There are times when a paddler just stops and stares, almost not believing that in Rhode Island an unspoiled shore could ever be so beautiful.

Looking south toward the mouth of the Sakonnet River from Fogland Beach, High Hill Point on the left (east) 0.7 NM away and Black Point on the right (west) 1.9 NM away frame the southernmost 5 NM of the river; Sachuest Point on the west side of the river's mouth can with difficulty be made out on the skyline behind Black Point.

Fogland Beach: Driving

Take RI 77 south through Tiverton; turn right onto Pond Bridge Road. Follow road until in sight of water, and turn right at sign for Fogland Beach. Do not go straight ahead to the boat ramp. Follow the road out along the beach.

Parking is permitted between the tarred road and the picnic tables, and launching should be possible even in season out of the way of swimmers.

Fogland Beach: Launching

About 0.7 NM south of Fogland Point, High Hill Point juts out from the western shore of Tiverton into the Sakonnet River; Fogland Point then protrudes even further out into the river *(fig. 117)*. North of Fogland Point the shoreline has retreated 0.5 NM to the east, close to the general line that it had south of High Hill Point. The next point of land to the north, 1.3 NM upstream, is Sapowet Point, which extends out more than 0.3 NM to the west from the straight shoreline that meets its southern side.

The embayment sheltered between Fogland and Sapowet Points is shaped like a parallelogram 1.3 NM long north to south and about 0.4

Fig. 117 *Outer part of Fogland Point from the south*

NM wide, with an average depth at low tide of around 12 feet. West of this parallelogram, the Sakonnet River channel angles from the opposite side of the river by Sandy Point to the near side, closely skirting Sapowet Point; just west of a line connecting the tips of Fogland and Sapowet Points, mean low-tide depths run as deep as 40–60 feet. The ebb current sweeps into the sheltered area from the north with about the strength it has out in the channel, but the flood current has less than half the speed inside the parallelogram as in the channel; the region between the two points is shielded better by Fogland than by Sapowet.

Barring heavy weather from the west or north, then, and preferably on a flood tide, a paddler who can get into this parallelogram has about a square mile of water and over a mile and a half of shoreline to investigate *(fig. 118)*.

Fig. 118 *Looking north from the north side of Fogland Point*

Watertrail 7B, Link 1: Fogland Point to Sapowet Point

Sachuest Point at the west side of the Sakonnet River's mouth draws in uncommon birds like a magnet, and Fogland Point seems to do the same: it took no effort at all to see an immature wheatear through the car windshield one morning in September. So, if you find the point almost deserted as you drive out and prepare to launch, holding down the ruckus may reward you with some unexpected encounters, possibly with wildlife that is far from local.

Launching from the south side should be easy, depending on the waves. The base of the point, that is, the beginning of the beach back toward the boat ramp, lies more in the shadow of High Hill Point and may offer easier launching if the surf zone farther out the beach is too lively.

Fogland and Sapowet Points and the straight and still-rural coastline between them are among the most appealing places in the bay. It may have been the clear, even slightly chilly day in early fall when the spartina's plumes had begun to gild the upper fringe of the shoreside grass that gave the view such splendor, but it also seemed to be a magical place: Fogland blanks out the tumult from the south, and for a distance you can race or swerve or coast beside the shore or farther off with a mile of river's breadth to the west and low-sloped cultured land gradually climbing up behind trees, beyond marsh grass and beaches on the east. Along this straight shoreline, too, are several stone piers, too carefully made to be breakwaters: "loading docks," you might call them; constructions such as these are not common through the bay, rare in fact, and to find two in good shape and the remains of a third

Fig. 119 *Between Fogland Point and Sapowet Point on the west bank of the Sakonnet River*

adds to your consciousness of being privileged still to be able to step with care through a last impossibly precious trace of Narragansett Bay as it must once have been. This isn't to say that no one lives along the shore; people always have. But the houses do not bully the landscape; they nestle instead of strut and so give the countryside they dwell in room to breathe *(fig. 119)*.

After a mile along the straight south-to-north shoreline you draw closer to the most visible landmark hereabouts, the bridge over Sapowet Creek. Remind yourself which way the tide is flowing, because, as seems to be characteristic of just about every place where water has a chance to enter or leave the Sakonnet River, the water does not dawdle beneath the bridge: Either it is rushing in or rushing out, perhaps faster than you can paddle *(fig. 120)*.

Sapowet Marsh on the inland side of the bridge is a nature preserve and should not be disturbed.

Fig. 120 *View from the bridge over Sapowet Creek along south-facing side of Sapowet Point*

Crossing the creek's current to Sapowet Point on an ebbing tide is good clean fun; the force of the outrushing water will succeed in turning your boat, perhaps even overturning it. The waves from the river, slowed and steepened as they encounter the shallows, topple when they collide against the outflow. You could probably touch bottom in these shallows if you reached with your hand over the side of your boat, if you had a hand to spare amid all the splashing and soaking going on. If your boat does tip over, scramble out and tow it over to the nearest sand spit sticking out from the beach. You might even want to go back and do it again. Be sure that all in your party have life jackets on and can handle a capsizing in the current.

Watertrail 7B, Launching Site 2: Sapowet Point Beach

Launching from the beach facing Sapowet Cove gives a paddler several choices of things to do, all of which are fun: Tussle with the outflow from Sapowet Marsh, cross over that and go south into the sheltered rectangle of water between Fogland and Sapowet Points, or go north around Sapowet to the bight behind Jack's Island.

The Sapowet Point Beach is simple to find and parking spaces are plentiful.

Sapowet Point Beach: Driving

Come south on RI 77 from Tiverton and turn right on Seapowet Road. Drive past the Emilie Ruecker Wildlife Sanctuary. The road will bend to the left. Continue until you reach the Sapowet Bridge; before the bridge, drive in to the right and park.

You can also drive south on RI 77 as before, but continue farther along and turn right onto East Road. This will bring you to the Sapowet Bridge as well; cross the bridge, turn left, and park.

Fishermen seem to use mostly the beaches near the bridge and the end of the point, so launching from the beach between the two sand spits along this shore seems least likely to interfere with other activities here.

Sapowet Point Beach: Launching

The fishing area and beach along the south side of Sapowet Point form a shore aligned along 310 degrees magnetic, and the north shore of the point tends toward 50 degrees magnetic; the two sides are joined by a tight curve around the point, giving Sapowet a broadly angular form reminiscent of High Hill Point and Church's Point farther south, although Sapowet cannot claim to have their elevation. Sapowet is a land of marshes, both at the base of the southern side and along the northern one as well. This northern shore faces a triangular cove bounded by Sapowet on the southeast, Nannaquaket Neck on the northeast, and the river's channel on the west. The broad mouth of this cove stretches north from Sapowet Point 1.3 NM before reaching the place where Nannaquaket Neck and the channel converge just south of the level of Gould Island. Strong tidal currents do not reach into this triangle, although just outside they move along at half a knot at times.

At the level of Sapowet Point the marked boat channel lies barely 250 yards from shore, with depths approaching 40 feet. It is a narrow channel, though, and a watchful scamper to the west for 0.4 NM should put a paddler into the large protected region north of McCorrie's Point that Watertrail 7A traverses.

The tips of Sapowet and Nannaquaket Points are 2.1 NM apart; the latter forms the southern side of the entrance into Nannaquaket Pond, which is a mile long and a quarter mile wide and, except for the entrance channel and a hollow dredged by the current on the pond side of the bridge that crosses where the pond begins, it is barely 3 feet deep at low tide.

Two-tenths NM north along the shore from the inlet to Nannaquaket Pond is Grinnell's Beach at the base of the remnants of the Old Stone Bridge on the eastern shore, the northern end of Watertrail 7B.

For relaxation, paddlers should stay well tucked in against the side of Nannaquaket Neck as they near its northern end and also close to shore north of the inlet to Nannaquaket Cove: The ebb tide current especially moves quickly here, reaching 0.7 knots downstream from Grinnell's Beach.

Watertrail 7B, Link 2:
Sapowet Point Beach to Grinnell's Beach

A tribe of semipalmated plovers, those immaculate and gentle-hearted little shorebirds, inhabits the south side of Sapowet Point, and a paddler who stays some boat lengths from the shore may spot them foraging among the small stones near the waterline; if they should be alarmed and fly away, repeat their whistled call and some or all of them will wheel around and set down where they were, apparently easily reassured.

As you emerge past the south side of Sapowet Point you'll at once feel the main tidal current tug at your boat, and the bottom here is a rocky jumble. It isn't necessary to swing far away from shore; just be alert here to the abruptness of the transition.

Sapowet Point is hollow, as are so many others in the bay, that is, a barrier beach outlines the point but lower marshy ground with a pond or two lies within. You will see the mouths of tidal brooks as you paddle along the west face of the point. American egrets seem always to be in the pond inside the barrier beach, and they also seem to be incapable of waiting out the passage of even a solo kayak: the sight of four large, brilliantly white birds lifting themselves out of the hollow on those great wings that gleam against the trees and then the sky always is enough to make one stop and watch, but also to worry what damage continual traffic, even light traffic, would do to their welfare. Perhaps in the future I'll skirt Sapowet Point farther from the shore *(fig. 121)*.

Fig. 121 *Southernmost stony shallows at the southwest corner of Sapowet Point on the Sakonnet River*

The water north of the point is sheltered once again from waves out in the river.

The north side of Sapowet Point bulges out as Jack's Island before it returns to the overall line of the Tiverton shore, and the paddler will see

Fig. 122 *Well-protected, one-boat slip along the north side of Sapowet Point*

inlets north and south of Jack's Island, that look tempting to explore *(fig. 122)*. The one northeast of the bulge, on the far side from Sapowet Point, though, leads into a wildlife sanctuary managed by the Rhode Island Audubon Society and should be regarded as off-limits. The sanctuary, however, can be visited by land and appreciated from its network of foot trails.

Moving up along the shore brings you past a mix of old and new houses, occasionally with a scenic combination of landscape and architecture *(fig. 123)*. After a half mile, though, the water is apt to demand more attention than the scenery. Waves that missed Sapowet Point find

Fig. 123 *Nannaquaket Neck in early autumn*

landfall here along Nannaquaket Neck and the 3-fathom line swings in to hug the steep shore, thanks to the dredging effect of the water that rushes south from Mount Hope Bay through the narrows, then straight through this sluiceway.

Waves here can be amusingly pyramidal as wave trains from several widely spread directions intersect. Rule of thumb along Nannaquaket Neck: Stay 50 yards or less from shore *(fig. 124)*.

Fig. 124 *Looking north along Nannaquaket Neck (at right)*

Gould Island provides a little cover after a while, and soon the bank at the paddler's right curves sharply in at the entrance to Nannaquaket Pond, the Quaket River, which embodies another instance of strong tidal flow in and out of the Sakonnet River. Judging from the way my kayak crawled upstream against an ebbing tide, the current at the bridge across the Quaket River can approach four knots; either getting in or out of Nannaquaket Pond is going to be easy but, unless you timed your passages for slack water, not both.

Avoid getting your boat's bow caught by the main current, if the current is ebbing and you wish to go to Grinnell's Beach. Paddle a way up toward the pond going close along the shore, and when you are close to the bend, nose left and head across; you'll be carried sideways, of course, but even with the twists as you pass through eddies, you should cross the current from the pond and find yourself well set up for the approach to Grinnell's Beach. This crossing may not be for the kids *(fig. 125)*.

Fig. 125 *Looking into the Quaket River from just inside the mouth's south side*

Fig. 126 *Grinnell's Beach, the north end of Watertrail 7B*

By the way, as you paddle north after crossing the Quaket River, look out for the boulder that sits almost dead ahead about halfway up to the beach.

Land anywhere along the beach, unless an area in season is set aside for swimmers, of course. Usually, too, you'd be safe in assuming that where gulls line the shore, no one is swimming in the water, but here you would be wrong, for a woman who swims here often has almost tamed the gulls. They seem to gather on the shore where she is bathing, so keep an eye open for her head in the water *(fig. 126)*.

Watertrail 7B, Launching Site 3: Grinnell's Beach

A paddler wishing to try Watertrail 7B starting at the north end will easily find Grinnell's Beach beside the road. Approach the water with some caution, however, and better yet with local information. There's the outflow from the Sakonnet River narrows to the right, the outflow from the Quaket River ahead and to the left (reverse direction of current to suit the tide), and water shown on charts as 81 feet deep between the beach and Gould Island.

Grinnell's Beach: Driving

From the north, from Fall River and I-195, come south on RI 24 (not RI 138) into Tiverton. Continue south beside the harbor briefly; Grinnell's Beach is on the right, at the eastern part of the Old Stone Bridge and marked by a sign. There's a gas station beside the turnoff and the expanse of the Sakonnet River is visible beyond the gas station.

Grinnell's Beach: Launching

The most important factor governing everyday paddling here is the state of the tide. The Sakonnet Narrows, and especially the constriction formed by the remaining abutments of the Old Stone Bridge, create a two-way nozzle that either draws in toward the north or jets out toward the south a healthy fraction of the water that enters and leaves Mount Hope Bay each tidal cycle; the maximum currents are substantial, especially on the ebb. The intervals of slack tide being brief and the currents locally offshore from the beach confusing, the paddler wishing to avoid excitement, and quite possibly danger, will slide along the shore of Grinnell's Beach heading downriver and approach the beach the same way.

Glossary

*T*HE GLOSSARY bears down on history and derivations. People have been calling out words that sound like "Starboard!," for example, for well over a thousand years as they, too, struggled against wind and waves.

If one ever needs convincing that the nautical vocabulary of Modern English has deep roots in the Germanic side of English language's ancestry and Old Norse in particular, a visit to a small harbor and a stint onboard a sailboat in Scandinavia should prove the point. Northern Germany and the Netherlands also demonstrate the similarities, but there's something about pronunciation in the Nordic countries that instantly sounds familiar. A "boat" is *båt* in Swedish, which sounds the same except for the vowel being a little deeper and longer; it is *Boot* in German, with pronunciation a little closer to the Swedish than the English. Our "ship" in Swedish is *skepp*," in which the "k" is not hard, like ours, but soft, somewhat like a "wh"; try it: It comes out sounding like a windy version of "shep." German has "*Schiff*," again, a little farther away from English.

Boats in General

bow: the front end of the boat. The word's origins are unclear, though they appear to stretch all the way back to the Indus River valley and a word meaning "forearm"; think of "elbow." In North Sea sailing ships the grain of the wood in each ship's timber followed the shape of the component; thus, in the keel (defined below) the long, straight section beneath the boat was cut from the straight trunk of a tree, often 60 feet in length, while the upward curving bow and stern sections must have come from a part of a tree either naturally

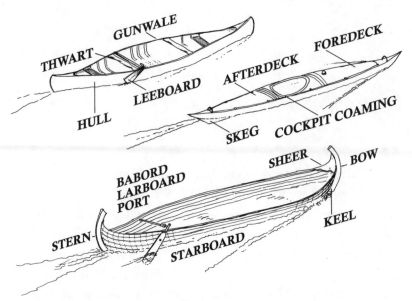

or artificially curved, either a "bough" (same root word) or conceivably a trunk or branch that grew while held in a "bowed" position.

stern: the back end of the boat. It comes from the Old Norse language word "*stjórn*," or the "steering end" of the boat, which is related to the verb "*styra*," or "to steer," which gave us "starboard" (see below).

hull: a Germanic word; the structural body of a boat, minus masts, seats, and so on. In the case of a canoe, essentially everything that gives it its shape. In the case of a kayak, "hull" is usually considered not to include the deck (defined below), regardless of the deck's contribution to a kayak's structural integrity. The shape of a boat's hull dictates much of its interaction with the water; in fact, you could argue that a boat's hull is that part of the boat that encounters clear water in the normal range of operations.

keel: in Old Nordic wooden ships, the sturdy timber that swept down from the bow aft along the bottom of the hull and up to the stern to define the hull's outline from the side. In a rowboat, often a simple strip of wood attached to the outside of a hull along its centerline both stiffens the bottom of the boat and protects it when drawn up on land. If there's a matching strip on the inside of the hull so that the bottom panels or planks of the boat are sandwiched between it and the keel, that piece is the "keelson," which is not derived from "son-of-keel" but "keel-swine" or "keel-pig," another curious moniker for a ship's timber. In a traditional canvas-covered wood canoe with internal ribs to support and shape the hull, the keel was fundamental to its construction; it also protruded below the hull to form a long, shallow ventral fin, which acted to reduce sideslip and to increase tracking. Accessory keels could be added parallel to the main keel but spaced to either side to increase tracking stiffness further. In a kayak, a keel is more a feature of the hull shape than a separate structural element.

deck: the surface that covers (most of) the cavity created by the hull. Typically, rowboats lack decks. Kayaks, not considering complications introduced by the sit-on-top variety, are completely decked over, save for cockpit openings to accommodate the paddler or paddlers. In early Nordic boats, the "*däck*" was removable flooring across the interior of the broad, shallow hull on which the crew walked and under which they stored their cargo and supplies; the removable lath flooring in some old wooden canoes might be considered a vestigial deck.

coaming: the raised, reinforced edge around a hatch or cockpit opening to keep out water and provide a rim where a hatch cover or, in the case of a kayak, a spray skirt can be fastened; thus, a kayak cockpit coaming has a lip around the outside edge. Apparently nothing is known about the origin of this term, but I find it suggestive that we call a breaking wave a "comber," sometimes "coamer," and that the crest of a breaking wave in Swedish is "*vågkam*," literally, the "wave-comb"; the coaming keeps out the "wave-comb."

babord: the left side of the boat or ship, looking forward. This is a trick: "*Babord*" is a Swedish word, not an English word, a combination of "bare" + "board," which is exactly its original meaning. The old wooden ships that sailed the Baltic and North Seas and beyond were built lengthwise of long, overlapping, cleverly shaped, and twisted planks, or "boards" as we might say. The ship's "bord" was the hull's outer sheathing, in particular the part above the water, or the "freeboard." The keel of such a ship swept up at both the bow and the stern in a long, graceful curve, and although on occasion the builders did attach a rudder to the hull's centerline at its curved stern, the shipbuilders far more often attached a large steering oar to the right side of the hull forward of the stern, choosing the right side because, like today, there were more right-handed skippers than left-handed ones. The left side of the hull was bare, "bar" to them, and hence was the "bar-bord" side, shortened to "babord."

starboard: the right side of the ship, the one (if you were sailing the North Sea) with the steering oar and thus the "steering-side" of the ship. Even in modern Swedish, "to steer" is "*styra*," and to a Swede, "starboard" is "*styrbord*."

larboard: like the Swedish "*babord*," the left side of the ship. If you were sailing the North Sea in a wooden ship with a steering oar, you most likely were on some sort of business trip: a little trading, a little plundering, a little more trading. You loaded and unloaded cargo over the side of the ship, probably as it was pulled up against a wharf, and not wanting to damage your steering oar, you placed the nonstarboard side, the bare babord side, against the rocks or pilings; *babord* functionally became the "loading-side." "To load" in Swedish is "*ladda*;" "*ladda-bord*" emerges in English as "larboard."

port: and again, the left side of the ship. Loading and unloading became more and more to be done in settled ports-of-call for these sea rovers, and the loading-side, or larboard, became also the port-side, as speakers of Romance languages contributed to English nautical terminology. Both terms persisted through the age of sail, but in English "port" has won out in the end, possibly because there's less chance of confusion between "port" and "starboard" than between "larboard" and "starboard" in commands. Swedish has kept the old "babord" and "styrbord" possibly because the "a" and "y" have such distinct sounds.

Canoes

gunwale: in old large wooden ships, the planking covering the heads of the hull timbers where they stood above the deck and on which guns used to be mounted. In a canoe or rowboat, the upper edge of the hull. Pronounced "gunnel" and sometimes spelled that way, too. The "-wale" part came from a word in the Old Norse language for "knuckle," which took on the meaning of "ridge," presumably a lumpy one (the "wale"—used for speaking about corduroy cloth—is the same word).

thwart: one of the structural members that lies across the length of the canoe and connects the gunwales. Apparently, the word is used in north Britain connoting "thought," "thaught," "thoft," and "thaft," meaning a rower's seat or bench and traced to an Old Norse root. (I was always told, however, not to sit on the thwarts in our family's wooden canoe.)

athwart: in the horizontal direction at a right angle to the length of the boat. Also, there's the similar term "abeam," but it's used to describe a position not on the boat; a buoy may come abeam.

leeboard: not to be confused with "larboard," a leeboard is a blade that can be lowered into the water on the lee side of a sailing canoe. Because sailing canoes often have a lot of sail for very little hull, they may be heeled far over, with the windward half of the hull nearly out of the water; such vessels need to have their underwater lateral area increased both for stability and to reduce sideslip. A centerboard could be installed, perhaps, but the canoe, when not sailing, would not be a canoe but something else with a tall housing in the center of the loading area: Leeboards allow one to have lateral area on demand without significantly modifying the canoe itself. Each end of a beam fastened thwartwise on top of the gunwales has a blade that can be swung into the water when needed and held in position by friction; that is, there's a port leeboard and a starboard leeboard. A canoe without a sail that found itself in strong winds on open water could benefit from available leeboards; its paddlers could both reduce sideslip and eliminate leecocking and weathercocking by dropping a leeboard from the optimal location along the lee gunwale.

Kayaks

cockpit: in a kayak, the volume in which a paddler sits. Any kayak used on the bay ought to have a sealed volume in which water cannot enter forward of, and behind, the cockpit; a cockpit must be large enough to keep kayak, paddler, and cargo afloat, even when it is filled with water.

sheer: the upward sweep of the deck, or of the upper profile of a vertical section through the boat, toward the bow and stern. The term "sheer plank" specifies the uppermost plank of a boat's hull sheathing. On old Nordic boats, the sheer plank had a very strong sheer both fore and aft. The sheer of a contemporary kayak is the line of the join between the hull and the deck; this term is preferred to "gunwale." In a wooden kayak, the sheer is set or reinforced by a molding that runs the entire length of the boat along the inside angle of this join, called the "sheer clamp." The fact that the side of the hull makes a vertical and uninterrupted, or sheer, drop from the boat's sheer seems to be regarded as an etymological accident, but the alternative explanations also seem no better; it must have been a long, straight, uninterrupted drop from the sheer of an 18th-century ship-of-the-line down to the water.

chine: between the sheer and the keel, the place where the profile of the hull, when seen in cross-section, transitions from vertical to more or less horizontal to meet the keel. The shorter the profile's radius of curvature in this region and the greater the change of direction, the "harder" the chine. The gentler the curve, the wider the angle, the "softer" the chine. Kayaks can have multiple chines, as though fabric were stretched over several longitudinal stringers. The term may come from the Scandinavian word "kind" (pronounced as

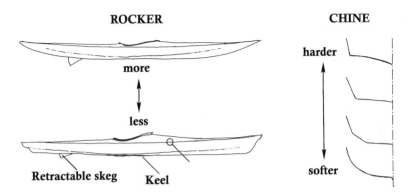

ROCKER **CHINE**

more

less

harder

softer

Retractable skeg Keel

something between "shind" and "whind"), which means "cheek," as though the sides of the boat were its cheeks.

skeg: a fillet that continues the mainly horizontal line of the keel to the kayak's stern as the hull itself rises to the waterline. It provides lateral area far back on the boat to improve tracking. The term also denotes a small fin, usually retractable, that can be dropped down through a slot in the keel somewhat forward of the stern and adjusted, ideally, to render the boat neutral in the wind. From the Scandinavian skägg (meaning "beard" and possibly originally denoting the considerable lateral area provided all along a Viking boat's length by the part of the keel that protrudes away from the hull planking), a protrusion particularly pronounced at the bow, where it added lateral area that was probably needed to balance the lateral area of the steering oar near the stern. The sense of "protrusion from a keel" remains the same.

rocker: the counterpart of "sheer," as the term describes how the bottom profile of the hull curves up at bow and stern. Imagine the rockers on a rocking chair having the profile of the kayak's keel. The more "rocker" on the boat the less lateral area below the waterline toward the ends of the boat and the less resistance to turning, thus, the greater the kayak's agility, although probably at some cost to tracking.

Wind, Tide, and Shore

weather: the *Oxford English Dictionary* opines that "weather" came long ago from the same Germanic language base that gave us the word "wind." In between we find *weder* in Old English and *ve(th)r* in Old Norse, and you can probably take your pick as to which gave us the modern word. The point is that on the water "weather" means "wind."

Into the Wind

weather side: the weather side of the boat is the side the wind is blowing against.

weather rail: heard more commonly than "weather side." On a sailboat, the crew might be asked to hike out over the weather rail in order to lessen the tilt, or heel, of the boat away from the wind to improve handling and increase speed or just to keep the boat from going over entirely

aweather: toward the weather side or into the wind. It is rarely used but is a perfectly good word

windward, upwind: "to windward" means "aweather"; "windward" and "upwind" are adjectives, like "weather."

Away from the Wind

lee: the most direct ancestor of "lee" is again one of the cultures that sailed the North Sea and the Baltic, as essentially the same word occurs in Old Norse and in German, probably from the northern coast; modern German also uses the word "Schutz" meaning "shield" as in "shielded from the wind," which, like much German technical terminology, is self-explanatory. In Swedish, the word is "*lä*," pronounced like our "lay" without the "ee" sound at the end and dragged out a bit.

alee, to leeward, downwind: the direction or side of the boat sheltered from the wind. An English speaker at the helm of a Swedish sailboat can say "Helm alee!" and the crew will know what is meant and also think that the skipper has been clever to learn the Swedish word and overlook what they suppose to be his mispronunciation of it.

lee shore: the land downwind from the boat, in the boat's lee. It represents a danger particularly to sailboats, which rely solely on the wind for propulsion and is worse yet for square-rigged vessels, which have trouble clawing their way upwind, if indeed they can do it at all. For a paddler, it is a matter of "it depends": It depends on whether the boat and paddler can prevail against the wind, on whether the lee shore would permit a soft landing, and so on. Being in the water beside a capsized kayak a short distance upwind of a rocky lee shore where strong waves are breaking is a ticklish situation.

in the lee of the land: where the wind is coming off the land toward the boat, and the land is shielding the boat from the wind's full force. Usually a good place to be.

A Boat's Reaction to the Wind

A weathervane is a gadget that pivots to point into the wind, also called a weathercock. British usage substitutes "fane" for "vane." Old Norse had "vani"; modern German has "Fahne," our "flag." The origins of our verb "to cock" in the sense of "to cock one's head" and "to cock a gun," from the days when you actually pulled back a hammer, seem obscure; the word, however, seems to connote rotation through a certain angle.

That is precisely what happens when a boat weathercocks or leecocks: The boat rotates, or yaws, either into or away from the wind and off the heading you want.

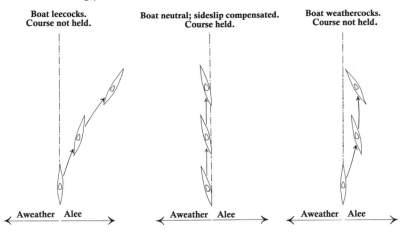

Boat leecocks. Course not held. — Boat neutral; sideslip compensated. Course held. — Boat weathercocks. Course not held.

Aweather Alee   Aweather Alee   Aweather Alee

weathercock: boat yaws aweather. In other words, with the wind blowing on the boat other than from straight ahead or behind, the boat wants to align itself facing into the wind. Since the bow of the boat is not actually managing to move upwind, this happens as the stern of the boat sideslips downwind more than the bow does.

leecock: boat yaws alee. The bow sideslips downwind more than the stern, and the boat wants to rotate so as to present its stern to the wind. A kayaker usually finds it easier to compensate for weathercocking than for leecocking; steering involves having a paddle blade in the water behind the cockpit, which adds lateral area at the rear of the boat and reduces the stern's tendency to sideslip still further, so worsening the leecocking.

(to) heel: for the boat to tilt toward its starboard or port side. If this is caused by the pressure of the wind coming from the side, then the boat will almost certainly heel so as to lower the lee side and raise the weather side. If the boat is so small that it responds to the slope of a wave, then heeling can be caused also by the boat's hull trying to keep each side equally immersed despite the fact that the water surface is not level. Too much heeling for either reason can cause the boat to assume a more stable position in which the boat is on top and the paddler is on the bottom. Apparently nothing is known about the origin of the word, although it seems it might share the ancient root of "wheel," "hjul" in Swedish, which had the meaning of "to rotate."

Index